The Freelance E

The Freelance Educator is the definitive resource for K-12 teachers who are ready to utilize their skills outside of the classroom and embark on a fast-paced, highly rewarding entrepreneurial journey.

Author Tinashe Blanchet, who has launched and managed two educational businesses, provides all the details you need to get started as an independent educational consultant. She uses a blend of her own experience, thorough research, and interviews with over 40 freelance educators to provide you with step-by-step advice. Topics covered include making the transition, finding your vision, establishing a legitimate business, branding and marketing, communicating with clients, making and managing your money, and growing your business. Each chapter is filled with interactive features to help you pause, reflect, and apply what you are learning.

With the helpful suggestions in this book, you'll be able to launch your new career, helping schools improve student outcomes, traveling around the world, meeting new people, and learning all along the way!

Tinashe Blanchet is a former high school math teacher with over 18 years of experience in education and teacher training. She is a Google for Education Certified Innovator and Trainer who has traveled around the United States to train thousands of teachers on using technology to enhance their instruction. Tinashe has built a strong reputation as a skilled communicator and tech-savvy educator and has presented at local, state, national, and international education conferences including ISTE and NCTM. Learn more about Tinashe and her work at msblanchet.net.

The Freelance Educator

Practical Advice for Starting Your Educational Consulting Business

Tinashe Blanchet

Routledge
Taylor & Francis Group

NEW YORK AND LONDON

Cover image: Hilary Allison

First published 2022
by Routledge
605 Third Avenue, New York, NY 10158

and by Routledge
4 Park Square, Milton Park, Abingdon, Oxon, OX14 4RN

Routledge is an imprint of the Taylor & Francis Group, an informa business

Library of Congress Cataloging-in-Publication Data
A catalog record for this title has been requested

ISBN: 978-1-032-00015-2 (hbk)
ISBN: 978-0-36777-170-6 (pbk)
ISBN: 978-1-00317-230-7 (ebk)

DOI: 10.4324/9781003172307

Typeset in Palatino
by Apex CoVantage, LLC

This book is dedicated to you, the reader. Your interest in starting an educational consulting business reflects your talent and skill as an educator and your courage as an aspiring entrepreneur. May you be inspired, excited, and well-informed by this text, which was written especially for you.

Contents

Acknowledgements

The author would like to acknowledge her children, Jade, Kwesi, and Nia Blanchet, who inspire her to do and be her best every single day.

She would also like to thank everyone who supported and encouraged her as she worked to complete this project, particularly Gabriel Arnold, Tanjanesia Willoughby, Audra Ryes, Joi Guillory, Marcus Stein, Michelle Blouin-Williams, Monica Pierre, Knikole Taylor, and Desiree Alexander.

To the freelance educators who agreed to be interviewed for this book, your expertise and wisdom are invaluable. Thank you for sharing your inspiring stories!

A final and sincere debt of gratitude is owed to illustrator Hilary Allison and editor Lauren Davis for your patience and professionalism as you collaborated with the author to make this book a reality.

Meet the Author

Tinashe Blanchet is a former high school math teacher with over 18 years of experience in education and teacher training. She is a Google for Education Certified Innovator and Trainer who has traveled around the United States to train thousands of teachers on using technology to enhance their instruction. Tinashe has built a strong reputation as a skilled communicator and tech-savvy educator and has presented at local, state, national, and international education conferences including ISTE and NCTM. With a Master's degree in Curriculum and Instruction, Tinashe has served as a non-profit founder and director, college instructor, and independent educational consultant. She is now a professional development specialist at Texthelp, a company that creates an award-winning suite of products that helps millions of people read, write, and research with confidence worldwide.

1

Beginning With Your WHY

The purpose of this book is to inform and empower K-12 educators who are interested in working independently as educational consultants, i.e., freelance educators. Educational consulting can be very rewarding, especially if you enjoy traveling, presenting, offering advice, and meeting new people. Most powerfully, independent educational consultants can expand their potential impact way beyond their own classroom, school or organization by using their expertise to empower educators, near and far, to improve their practice.

DOI: 10.4324/9781003172307-1

According to the Indeed Career Guide,

> An educational consultant is a professional with training and relevant degrees who offers feedback and suggestions to other education professionals like teachers and administrators, as well as parents and children. As an educational consultant, you will work to become an expert in your field and then use that expertise to assist others in the field with improving their performance as educators. You may work with K-12 schools or universities or the students attending those schools, depending on your area of expertise. Many educational consultants have a background as a teacher or other educational professional.
>
> (Indeed Editorial Team, 2021)

College Board consultant Carolyn Fruin also writes:

> Educational consultants do many things. They advise K-12 school districts on how to integrate technology into the classroom. They design and manage higher education and professional development programs for K-12 teachers at universities and colleges, [a]nd they help companies design products for teachers.
>
> (2015)

Do Now: Begin With Your WHY

Educators often begin a lesson plan with a list of objectives to answer the question: "what do I want my students to learn?" Similarly, your educational consultancy should also be driven by a strong sense of purpose. The most important first step you can take on a path towards starting any endeavor, but especially a business, is to really search your mind and heart to answer a very simple question:

WHY Am I Doing This?

Spend some time thinking about your response to this fundamental question and record your answer in writing, preferably in a digital format, so you will not misplace it. Think of writing and editing your WHY like writing "student-friendly" objectives. Your WHY, which can also be referred to as your business's mission statement, should be written as clearly and succinctly as possible, so that it is easy for you to communicate it to prospective clients, colleagues and other stakeholders. Your WHY will inform every facet of your consultancy, so take your time and do not hesitate to revise or rewrite it. As your consultancy evolves over time, so will your WHY.

⊘ Check for Understanding: Quitting Your Job Is Not a Good WHY!

There are many reasons why people choose to start a business. Many folks have a very clear vision of the kind of entity they want to build. Others may not know exactly what they want to do with their new enterprise, but they know that they are done with their current job or position. To be clear, quitting your job is neither a purpose nor is it a compelling reason to invest the time and significant effort required to build a successful educational consulting business. Instead, you may want to add leaving your full-time gig to pursue your business to a list of secondary goals or anticipated milestones.

Additionally, your WHY should not simply list your skills and/or services. While these can be included, be sure to stay purpose-driven with your mission statement. What will motivate you to keep doing the work even when you are faced with the inevitable challenges of starting and running a business? For example, if you have a passion for working with preschoolers, make sure your WHY reflects this. Perhaps you love figuring out ways to help students with behavior issues or special needs. Find a way to incorporate that into your mission statement.

Your WHY connects your skills and services to what you love to do or what you really believe in – your passion. Don't know where to start? Check out the following list of mission statements, with the WHY italicized, for some inspiration:

- ◆ I help people and organizations create, build, and expand *high quality early learning environments for young children*. I specialize in professional development, organizational administration, and leadership development. – Eboni Walker, Learning Matters LLC
- ◆ Susan Fitzell, M.Ed., CSP, knows how to bridge the organizational learning gap. Susan provides unique solutions that *transform performance by teaching people how they learn*. She helps leaders understand how to motivate and engage their employees.
- ◆ Educator Alexander Consulting, LLC *empowers educators to actualize becoming innovators and leaders*.
- ◆ *Positive, proactive solutions for working with challenging behaviors*: I work with educators of all grade levels, parents, legal professionals, and businesses. – Kathryn Phillips, Total Behavior Management

WHY "The Freelance Educator"?

The author of "The Freelance Educator," Tinashe Blanchet, is a former high school math teacher with over 18 years of experience in education. She is a freelance educator in her own right, who has worked independently as an educational technology consultant since 2013, training thousands of teachers as a Google-Certified Innovator and Trainer in more than 70 cities in over 40 states and abroad. Surprisingly, the question she was asked the most is totally unrelated to the topics on which she trained educators: "How did you get into this?" Whether she was training teachers in Hawaii or Canada, New Orleans or New Jersey, she was almost always approached by someone who wanted to know how they could break into a career in educational consulting.

The author's research revealed that there are many resources available for individuals to learn more about educational consulting, including books, articles, and videos. There are also lots of books and other resources available for starting a small business or even a consultancy. However, what she did not find was a step-by-step, how-to guide written particularly for K-12 educators who are interested in working independently as educational consultants.

About This Book

Based on her own experience and a great deal of research, the author has written what she hopes to be a powerful, easy-to-use resource for teachers who want to learn more about starting an educational consulting business. She also had the privilege to interview over 40 freelance educators, who graciously agreed to share their experience and expertise with the readers of this book. Each of the upcoming chapters begin with specific, practical advice shared by these educational consultants, from those who are just starting their business to experts with over 30 years of experience in the field. See Table 1.1 for a list of the names and consultancies of the freelance educators interviewed for this text.

In Table 1.2, you will find a chapter list as well as a brief description of what is covered in each.

See Table 1.3 for a list of "teacher-friendly" activities and featured content you will find in each of these chapters.

Every chapter also includes a cartoon infographic drawn by Hilary Allison. Hilary is a talented illustrator whose work has been featured in myriad publications, including The New Yorker. She has a knack for taking complex information and presenting it in a fun, easy-to-understand graphic format.

Table 1.1 The Freelance Educator Interviewee List

Name	Business Name (if applicable)
Dr. Desiree Alexander	Educator Alexander Consulting
Patricia Brown	Msedtechie Consultants LLC
Dave Burgess	Dave Burgess Consulting
Leticia Citizen	Tech.Teach.Grow, LLC
Kevin Curtis	National Educators for Restorative Practices
Vicki Davis	Cool Cat Teacher LLC
Cicely Day	Tech.Teach.Grow
Dr. Will Deyamport	The Dr. Will Show, The Edupreneur
Wendy Durant	DuraCARE
Josue Falaise	GOMO Educational Services
Susan Fitzell	Suan Fitzell and Associates
Savanna Flakes	Inclusion for a Better Future
Ariana Flewelling	
Mandy Frochlich	Mandy Froehlich Education Consulting, LLC
Jeff Gargas	Teach Better Team
Dr. Yvelyne Germain-McCarthy	
Catherine Halliwell-Templin	
Angela Hill	Carpe Diem Consulting Services LLC
Dr. Mary Howard	
Jin-Soo Huh	Baewoo Consulting LLC
Dr. Sawsan Jaber	Education Unfiltered Consulting
Rosalinda Jaimes	TechFairies
Frank Koontz	Bureau of Education and Research
Krista Leh	Resonance Education Inc
Tara Linney	TL Specialists LLC
Laurie Molnar	Learning Keys 21
Tammy Musiowsky-Borneman	Plan Z Professional Learning Services
Kathryn Phillips	Total Behavior Management
Rachelle Dené Poth	ThriveinEDU LLC
Dr. Natasha Rachell	Natasha Rachell, LLC
Dr. Julene Reed	Dr. Julene Reed Consulting
Lisa Rogers	Educating Diverse Learners
Tovi Scruggs-Hussein	Tici'ess, Inc.
Jim Sill	Deploy Learning

Name	Business Name (if applicable)
John Sowash	Sowash Ventures, LLC
Dr. John Staley	
Knikole Taylor	Knikole Taylor Learning Services
Dr. Sarah Thomas	Edumatch
Taneesha Thomas	Flutter Tech LLC
Dan Tricarico	The Zen Teacher
Dr. Mark Wagner	EdTechTeam, Inc.
Eboni Walker	Learning Matters LLC

Table 1.2 Chapter List With Descriptions

Chapter # and Title		Chapter Description
2	Writing a Business Plan	Guidance for both fledgling and experienced business owners, who may not currently have a business plan or may need to update and/or revise their existing one, with research-based activities, detailed templates, and online tools
3	Launch Your Educational Consulting Business	Learn all about launching an educational consulting business, including ways to actually start working and building an independent consultancy
4	Establishing Your Business (Paperwork + Incorporation)	Detailed information on establishing your business as a recognized entity by your stakeholders, the state you live in, and the Internal Revenue Service
5	Making + Managing Your Money	Overview of what it means to make and manage your money as an educational consultant, including budgeting advice, sample language to include in contracts and proposals, and guidance for opening a bank account and minimizing tax debt
6	Branding + Marketing	How to brand and market your business, including a list of six recommended items to meet your business's marketing needs
7	Communication + Project Management	Strategies for educational consultants to communicate effectively on behalf of their business and properly monitor client relationships from initial contact to rendering of services
8	Why + How to Grow Your Business	Advice for independent educational consultants who have built their business up to a point where they realize that they may need some help and strategies to increase your income and impact while focusing on existing clients

Table 1.3 "Teacher-Friendly" Activities and Featured Content

Do Now	Activities for you to put what you have learned in immediate practice. Do Nows appear throughout the chapter.
Exit Ticket	The Exit ticket is presented at the end of each chapter.
Extra Credit	Additional tasks designed to enhance some Do Nows and Exit Ticket activities
Check for Understanding	Information presented to address common misconceptions and frequently asked questions
Tech Tip	Free and low-cost digital tools useful for streamlining business tasks and reducing paperwork
Chapter Review	A brief synopsis or final thought for each chapter

Chapter Review: Written Just for You

Whether you are only thinking of becoming a freelance educator, just getting started with your business, or already working in the field, the information presented in the upcoming chapters will be relevant and helpful for you. Feel free to read this book from cover to cover, skim it, or just skip to the part that reflects your particular interests and needs. This book is written to be highly informative, relatable, and applicable, including many specific examples and research-based strategies. If you are a current or former K-12 teacher, then *The Freelance Educator* is written just for you!

Reference List

Fruin, Carolyn. (2015, 19 July). From the Classroom to Consultant in 6 Smart Steps. *EdSurge*, www.edsurge.com/news/2015-07-19-from-the-classroom-to-consultant-in-6-smart-steps.

Indeed Editorial Team. (2021, 12 March). How to Become an Educational Consultant. *Indeed*, www.indeed.com/career-advice/finding-a-job/how-to-become-an-educational-consultant.

2

Writing a Business Plan

Kathryn Phillips is an international speaker, author, teacher, and behavior expert who has worked in schools for over 35 years and leads Total Behavior Management (totalbehaviormanagement.com). Kathryn decided to write a business plan for her company two years after she started. She believes that, like her, many educators hesitate to put together a formal business plan when they transition to working independently. As a matter of fact, many of the educational consultants interviewed for this book reported that they do not currently have a business plan because they feel overwhelmed by it or they do not know where to start. Nevertheless, just like Kathryn, who eventually realized that she wanted a business plan to help her get more focused, any business owner could benefit from the process of writing one. When asked about the importance of a business plan for independent educational consultants, she stated simply: "It is a business, so a business plan is required . . . it's almost like an IEP for my business."

An IEP for Your Business

What an apt metaphor Kathryn shared – "an IEP for my business"! It makes sense for her to put it this way; much of her experience and expertise relates to children receiving special education and related services. As public K-12 school teachers in the United States should know, an IEP, or an Individualized Education Program, is a federally mandated document that is compiled by stakeholders in a child's education to detail his or her special needs and

DOI: 10.4324/9781003172307-2

present a clear, organized plan for how to address them. Among many other items, IEPs include a student's present levels of educational performance, annual goals, and short-term objectives or benchmarks. IEPs also list services to be provided to address the child's needs, and when, where, and for how long the services will take place (U.S. Department of Education, 2019). Like an IEP, an effective business plan requires its authors to:

◆ Thoroughly assess the present conditions and identify specific ways to improve them
◆ Set some reasonable short and long-term goals
◆ Articulate a plan to accomplish these goals in sufficient detail for clear communication with stakeholders and seamless implementation

To simplify the process detailed above even more, writing a business plan can be as easy as figuring out the answers to three essential questions that will be explored deeply in this chapter:

1 WHAT do you want to do?
2 WHY do you want to do this?
3 HOW will you get this done?

Why You Need a Business Plan

According to data from the Bureau of Labor Statistics, about 20%, or one out of every five, small businesses fail in their very first year. Alarmingly, this portion increases to a whopping 50% within the first five years. To put it plainly, if two friends start educational consulting businesses around the same time, according to the available data, one friend will be shuttering his or her business within five years. (McIntyre, 2020)

Consider the following scenario:

You work in a school as a teacher. You and the teacher across the hall from you will be observed by the principal tomorrow. Only one of you gets to write and use a lesson plan for the class in which you will be observed. Based on the quality and student outcomes of this lesson, only one of you will get to keep your job, i.e., someone will be fired.

Would you want to be the teacher who does not get to write a lesson plan in this scenario? If you do get to write one, how seriously would you take this

task? Would you write a basic, bare-bones plan or would you try to include as many details as possible?

As the old adage goes: "If you fail to plan, then you plan to fail." Teachers write lesson plans to list desired student outcomes, formulate classroom activities, and assess mastery of the skills presented in the lesson. Teachers create great lessons by beginning with the end in mind. This is also true about establishing a successful business.

☑ Check for Understanding: Starting With a Template

According to the U.S. Small Business Administration (SBA), a traditional business plan includes the following:

◆ Executive summary
◆ Company description
◆ Market analysis
◆ Organization and management
◆ Service or product line
◆ Marketing and sales
◆ Funding request
◆ Financial projections

This list is not only potentially overwhelming, but it also includes several elements that a fledgling consultancy may be unable or unmotivated to articulate in its early development. It would be premature for any new businessperson to try to complete a traditional business plan in detail before taking the time to formulate a much more general idea of what they seek to accomplish. After one is clear about how they want their business to look, they may realize that they are ready to complete a plan with this level of specificity. But, this is not the only option. Even the SBA offers an alternative "Lean startup plan" that is much simpler than the traditional format and can be completed in as little as one hour on a single page. (U.S. Small Business Administration, n.d.)

Templates can be highly effective in helping to organize one's thoughts. However, this begs the question: what are your thoughts? Rather than going to the SBA website or any other website or resource to grab a template, start the business planning process by figuring out exactly what you want. This will not only inform which template you choose, but it will also help you pick the specific template elements that make sense for you. You may even decide to go rogue and make your own template!

WHAT Do You Want?

Answering the question "what do you want?" in a detailed manner with regards to your business is the first critical step to writing a business plan. Take as much time as you need to figure out exactly what you want. Spend some time fantasizing about what your dream business would look like. Here is a (partial) list of questions to consider:

- What exactly would you be doing?
- Who are your dream clients?
- Where are you working? Are you going into schools and organizations or are they coming to you? Are you working in an office or from home?
- How much money would you like to make?
- Are you working alone or with a team?

Do Now: Dare to Dream!

Give yourself at least 15 minutes to come up with a clear vision, in your mind's eye, of what your ideal business would look and feel like. Write down as much of what you envision as you can. Treat this like a brainstorming exercise – do not worry about complete sentences or correct grammar. Just capture as much as possible. You can use this as a reference tool when you finally write a formal business plan.

Extra Credit: Make a Vision Board for Your Business

Vision boards are a great way to put together your thoughts and aspirations in a fun, informal, and visually appealing way. Constructed on poster paper or stretched canvas (for a more durable product), made of magazine clippings, printed images, and quotations, your vision board can be hung in your office or home as a constant reminder of the direction you want your business to go in.

Short on time? Make a mini-vision board! Buy a small canvas or use a regular sheet of typing paper as your backdrop. Even a small vision board can help you get focused. Your vision board may be small, but your vision is huge!

Figure 2.1 Author's latest vision board on canvas. This vision board is not limited to business, but includes it!

Source: Photograph by the author.

Figure 2.2 Author's mini vision board on canvas.

Source: Photograph by the author.

Tech Tip: Make a Digital Vision Board

A digital vision board can be created using an online tool like Google Jamboard (jamboard.google.com), Pinterest (pinterest.com) or Trello (trello.com). Although you may not see your digital board as much, since you would not pass by it in your home or office, an online board is much easier to update and edit. Also consider that you will have access to all the images and quotes on the web in addition to your own typed notes and/or drawings and uploaded images. You may also add dynamic, interactive media to your online vision board including videos, web links and animated images.

Figure 2.3 Author's digital vision board made with Google Jamboard.

Infusing Your WHY Into Your Vision

In the first chapter of this book, readers are encouraged to "Begin with your WHY." Once you take the time to clearly envision what your dream business would look like, interrogate this vision through the lens of your WHY. In other words, is your vision consistent with your mission? Is what you want to do completely aligned with what you want to accomplish? If not, that's okay. It simply means it is time to make some adjustments.

Aligning your vision with your WHY is very important, primarily because your business's reputation depends on it. Your integrity will be compromised if stakeholders observe that your business operates in ways that are inconsistent with your stated mission or purpose. For example, others may question your company's purported commitment to serving educators, if all of your offerings are priced at a level that makes them inaccessible to the average teacher, who has a limited salary.

If your overall goal is to provide much-needed support for schools and educators, but you also want your business to be highly lucrative, then you need to think deeply about how these two priorities can coexist. One way to connect these two seemingly competing interests is to offer free teacher training as a community service. This training can also serve as a marketing strategy to funnel more paying clients towards you. You could require free event participants to sign up for your mailing list, where you share opportunities for paid events in the future. Free events, especially ones that are informative and interesting, can attract lots of leads, some of which will convert to paid engagements. It is not about changing what you want, but figuring out how it all can work together.

In general, it is better to adjust your WHAT (vision) to match your WHY (mission), not vice versa. Beginning with your WHY is critical to ensuring that your work is fulfilling and worthwhile, especially when you encounter struggles in your business, which are inevitable. Like teaching, educational consulting is a challenging, yet rewarding profession for individuals who are motivated by a deeper purpose, such as helping teachers reach their students. Your WHY is what keeps you going, and that is unlikely to change. WHAT you do is essentially a matter of logistics and expertise, and can always be adapted to the different situations you face. Don't let logistics take you too far away from why you started your business in the first place!

Do Now: WHY v. WHAT Worksheet

Grab a sheet of paper (or open a document on your computer) and divide it into two columns titled "WHY" and "WHAT." In the WHY column list the reasons why you want to start your business. Which of your skills and/or talents do you want to utilize? Who do you want to help and how? In the WHAT column, list the services you want to provide. Be sure to use a pencil if you are working on paper. After you have two lists, go back and make the necessary edits to ensure that your WHAT aligns with your WHY.

HOW It All Comes Together

Now that you know WHAT you want, and you ensured that it is perfectly aligned with your WHY, it is now time to figure out exactly HOW you are going to accomplish what you decided to do. This sounds daunting, but it doesn't need to be. Like the business plan itself, the HOW part of business planning can be as simple or as complex as you desire. Keeping it simple means setting a few goals, deciding when you want to accomplish them, and who you may need to reach out to for help to get things done.

It is easy to confuse the HOW and WHAT aspects of this model so consider:

- ◆ WHAT includes exactly what you plan to do:
  - – The tasks that make up your daily work

  – Where it will be done
  – The audience for that work
◆ HOW includes the manner in which your work will be done:
  – How will you measure the quality of your work
  – How long will it take you to do your work
  – Who will help you get the work done

Something Is Better Than Nothing

Throughout the business planning process, remember the mantra: "*Something is better than nothing*." Educators know that this motto is not always true. Students often offer the most ridiculous answers to teacher questions simply to break the silence or to not leave a question unanswered. In this case, most teachers would prefer an "I don't know" to a random guess. However, "I don't know" is never the answer you want to give when asked about your business plan. It would be better to offer a simple, "elevator-pitch"-type answer than no answer at all. To this end, the first business plan template is one designed for you to get completed in one sitting:

FREElance Educator Bare-Bones Business Plan

The FREElance Educator Bare-Bones Business Plan is a quick and easy template that presents your business plan as answers to the three essential questions presented in this chapter:

1 WHAT do you want to do?
2 WHY do you want to do this?
3 HOW will you get this done?

Table 2.1 Bare-Bones Business Plan Template

1	WHAT do you want to do? What's your vision? Describe your dream business in a detailed paragraph.
2	WHY do you want to do this? What's your mission? How, specifically, does your vision align with what you hope to accomplish?
3	HOW will you get this done? What are your goals? When do you want to achieve them? Who will help you?

This plan is great for beginners, as it helps one to articulate their vision, mission, and goals without spending a lot of time listing details. This simple plan can also help experienced business owners develop an elevator pitch that is not overwhelming when presented to potential clients, collaborators, and other stakeholders.

Earlier in this chapter, the following scenario and questions were presented:

> *You work in a school as a teacher. You and the teacher across the hall from you will be observed by the principal tomorrow. Only one of you gets to write and use a lesson plan for the class in which you will be observed. Based on the quality and student outcomes of this lesson, only one of you will get to keep your job, i.e., someone will be fired.*
>
> *Would you want to be the teacher who does not get to write a lesson plan in this scenario? If you do get to write one, how seriously would you take this task? Would you write a basic, bare-bones plan or would you try to include as many details as possible?*

How did you answer the last question? Recall that a new educational consulting business has a 50–50 chance of survival after five years. As you probably would not want to write a bare-bones lesson plan if your teaching job depended on it, you also should not proceed with a bare-bones business plan, if you want your business to survive past five years. (McIntyre, 2020)

Consequently, below you will find a more detailed template for your business plan that integrates the simple WHAT, WHY, HOW model, but requires much more thought, planning and of course, time. But, remember, *something is better than nothing*. Feel free to use the bare-bones template to get started. You will probably want to expand it into a more detailed plan at a later date.

FREElance Educator Business Plan Builder

The FREElance Educator Business Plan Builder is designed to be a working document. You probably will not finish it in one sitting, and that is okay. It is also fine if you decide that certain elements are not necessary to include in your plan right away. Elements that you omit now may need to be added later. You may even come up with additional unique elements based on your specific business model.

Table 2.2 Business Plan Builder Template

WHAT (vision)	Company Description/Vision
	Services and/or Products
WHY (mission)	Industry/Market Analysis
	Target Audience/Ideal Client
	Mission Statement
HOW (goals)	Short-Term Goals
	Long-Term Goals
	Organization and Management
	Marketing and Sales Strategies
	Financial Projections

Below, you will find guidance on what to include in each section of the Business Plan Builder. Sections highlighted with an asterisk* are described with direct quotes from the SBA traditional business plan format, which can be found online at www.sba.gov/business-guide/plan-your-business/write-your-business-plan. (U.S. Small Business Administration, n.d.)

Company Description/Vision*

Use your company description to provide detailed information about your company. Go into detail about the problems your business solves. Be specific, and list out the consumers, organization, or businesses your company plans to serve. Explain the competitive advantages that will make your business a success. Are there experts on your team? Have you found the perfect location for your store? Your company description is the place to boast about your strengths.

Services and/or Products*

Describe what you sell or what service you offer. Explain how it benefits your customers and what the product life cycle looks like. Share your plans for intellectual property, like copyright or patent filings. If you're doing research and development for your service or product, explain it in detail.

Industry/Market Analysis*

You'll need a good understanding of your industry outlook and target market. Competitive research will show you what other businesses are doing and what their strengths are. In your market research, look for trends and themes. What do successful competitors do? Why does (or doesn't) it work? Can you do it better? Now's the time to answer these questions. (U.S. Small Business Administration, n.d.)

This part of your business plan can be daunting. It requires some research to determine what kind of work is being done in your field, and why your business needs to exist. Homeschooling Consultant, Teresa Roper, included a thorough analysis of her industry in her business plan for Quantum Education Services:

> The homeschooling industry includes educational companies that develop and market a variety of curricula, as well as consultants, national and state associations, publications, and homeschool groups. Following are some of the key industry players:

> ### National Organizations

> For homeschooling consultants and other industry players, one source of valuable information about the industry is the non-profit National Home Education Research Institute (www.nheri.org). According to the institute, which was established by Brian D. Ray, Ph.D., in 1990, the organization "conducts and collects research about homeschooling (home-based education, home schooling), and publishes the research journal called the *Home School Researcher*. The institute has hundreds of research works documented and catalogued on homeschooling, many of which were done by NHERI." Another leading national organization is the Home School Legal Defense Association (www.hslda.org), which supports "families whose right to homeschool is being challenged or discriminated against by school officials, social workers, employers, colleges, armed services recruitment officers, and government bureaucrats." Membership benefits offered by the HSLDA include access to lawyers and veteran homeschooling parents. In addition, the organization advocates for homeschool-friendly state and federal legislation.

> ### State Organizations

> The homeschooling industry also benefits from a large number of organizations operating at the state level. A list of these organizations

is available at http://teachinghome.com/states/index.cfm. For example, in Quantum Education Services' home state of Georgia, homeschooling participants have access to the Georgia Home Education Association.

Publications

Publications serving the homeschooling industry include the magazine, *Homeschooling Today* (http://homeschoolingtoday.com), which in addition to providing assistance and encouragement to families offers benefits such as practical activities and lessons. Another useful resource is *Practical Homeschooling Magazine* and the related Web site, Homeschool World (www.home-school.com), which enjoys a readership of more than 100,000 people.

(Greenland, 2017, 37–38)

Target Audience/Ideal Client

Who do you want to reach with your business? List each individual or entity that you seek to serve. In his blog post, "Choose your customers first," marketing expert Seth Godin writes: "first figure out who you'd like to do business with, then go make something just for them. The more specific the better" (Godin, 2013).

Take the time to describe in detail, who your ideal client is. What is their profession? What problems do they have that you are positioned to solve? How do they spend their free time? Do this for each individual client persona you wish to serve. The more time you invest in this endeavor, the more prepared you will be to attract and meet the specific needs of your clients.

Mission Statement

Your mission statement is essentially your WHY. Informed by your industry/market analysis and target audience/ideal client, describe the impact your business will have and/or what problem your business solves. For example, the author's mission statement for the non-profit organization she founded in 2014, The Learning Laboratory New Orleans, is as follows: "The Learning Laboratory is a diverse community of learners who engage in and create innovative educational experiences driven by passion and curiosity" (The Learning Laboratory New Orleans, n.d.). A good mission statement succinctly presents your business's priorities, who they will affect and how.

Short-Term Goals

List a few very specific milestones or achievements you want to accomplish in the next five years. Keep this list short, i.e., keep this list doable. The overall goal is to meet as many of these milestones as possible, so if they are too ambitious, they will exist only in your plan, and not in real life.

In her business plan for Bedford Childhood Development Consulting, Susan Bedford established the following strategy for years one – three:

Year One

Focus on building awareness about Bedford Child Development Consulting among professionals and families in the Rochester market. Begin operations with a core offering of 7 training programs for professionals. Secure 15 public speaking engagements. Generate gross revenue of $150,000 and net income of $7,500.

Year Two

Continue generating awareness about Bedford Child Development Consulting throughout Rochester. Develop an additional 5 training programs and secure 20 public speaking engagements, including one keynote address at a regional conference. Generate gross revenue of $165,000 and net income of $9,975.

Year Three

Continue to expand the business's educational/content offerings through the development of an additional 5 training programs. Secure 25 public speaking engagements, including one keynote address at a national conference. Begin evaluating the feasibility of hiring an additional early child development consultant, with specialized expertise in Down Syndrome, to expand the scope of advocacy services and training programs provided by the business. Generate gross revenue of $180,000 and net income of $9,950.

(Greenland, 2018, 79)

Long-Term Goals

What exactly do you want your business to look like in the distant future? Based on your answer to this question, list several goals you want to achieve in the long term. Keep these goals broad, as they will probably need to be changed over time. Do not worry about feasibility, as that is more appropriate for short-term planning. This is your opportunity to dream BIG!

Organization and Management*

How will your company be structured and who will run it? Describe the legal structure of your business. State whether you have or intend to incorporate your business as a C or an S corporation, form a general or limited partnership, or if you're a sole proprietor or LLC. Use an organizational chart to lay out who's in charge of what in your company. Show how each person's unique experience will contribute to the success of your venture. Consider attaching resumes and CVs of key members of your team.

Marketing and Sales Strategies*

There's no single way to approach a marketing strategy. Your strategy should evolve and change to fit your unique needs. Your goal in this section is to describe how you'll attract and retain customers. You'll also describe how a sale will actually happen. You'll refer to this section later when you make financial projections, so make sure to thoroughly describe your complete marketing and sales strategies.

Financial Projections*

If your business is already established, attach income statements, balance sheets, and cash flow statements for the last three to five years. If you have other collateral you could put against a loan, make sure to list it now.

Provide a prospective financial outlook for the next five years. Include forecasted income statements, balance sheets, cash flow statements, and capital expenditure budgets. For the first year, be even more specific and use quarterly – or even monthly – projections. Make sure to clearly explain your projections. This is a great place to use graphs and charts to tell the financial story of your business.

Grayson Noble shared his financial projections in his business plan for Noble Communications:

Projected Revenue, Expenses, and Net Income: 2021–2025

Revenue	2021	2022	2023	2024	2025
Speaking Engagements	$ 13,500	$ 24,750	$ 39,000	$ 56,250	$ 76,500
Book Sales	$ 0	$ 0	$ 7,500	$ 15,000	$ 22,500
Blog Advertising	$ 0	$ 0	$ 0	$ 2,500	$ 5,000
Total Revenue	**$13,500**	**$24,750**	**$46,500**	**$73,750**	**$104,000**
Expenses					
Salary	$ 5,000	$ 10,000	$ 25,000	$ 45,000	$ 65,000
Payroll Tax	$ 750	$ 1,500	$ 3,750	$ 6,750	$ 9,750
Accounting & Legal	$ 750	$ 1,500	$ 2,000	$ 2,500	$ 2,750
Office Supplies	$ 75	$ 150	$ 300	$ 375	$ 400
Equipment	$ 0	$ 500	$ 750	$ 750	$ 750
Marketing & Advertising	$ 2,500	$ 3,500	$ 5,500	$ 6,500	$ 7,500
Telecommunications & Internet	$ 1,000	$ 1,000	$ 1,000	$ 1,000	$ 1,000
Subscriptions & Dues	$ 0	$ 0	$ 450	$ 500	$ 550
Software Licenses	$ 150	$ 160	$ 170	$ 180	$ 190
Misc.	$ 400	$ 450	$ 500	$ 450	$ 500
Total Expenses	**$10,625**	**$18,760**	**$39,420**	**$64,005**	**$ 88,390**
Net Income	**$ 2,875**	**$ 5,990**	**$ 7,080**	**$ 9,745**	**$ 15,610**

Exit Ticket: Bare-Bones to Business Plan Builder Online Form

Visit bit.ly/freelanceedubusinessplan to create a bare-bones business plan using Google Forms. Once you submit the completed form, you will receive a business plan builder template that includes what you submitted and all of the elements in Table 1.2. This template is an editable Google Document that you can use to write a detailed, customized plan. If you prefer using Microsoft

Word, click "File"> "Download" > "Microsoft Word (docx)." Remember to feel free to add or remove any elements of the plan that make sense for you and your business.

Chapter Review: A Work in Progress

Even if you complete each section of the Business Plan Builder in detail, you should always view your business plan as a work in progress. As you accomplish your goals, you can add new ones. Over time, you may also choose to expand and/or adapt the scope of your vision and mission. A great business plan evolves as your business evolves. As long as your business exists, your business plan will never be truly finished!

Reference List

Godin, S. (2013, March 13). Choose Your Customers First. *Seth's Blog*. https:// seths.blog/2013/03/choose-your-customers-first/

Greenland, P. (2017). Homeschooling Consultant. In *Business Plans Handbook* (Vol. 38, pp. 37–42). Gale.

Greenland, P. (2018). Early Childhood Development Specialist/Consultant. In *Business Plans Handbook* (pp. 75–80). Gale.

The Learning Laboratory New Orleans. (n.d.). Mission. *What We Do*. www. lrnlabnola.org/what-we-do

McIntyre, G. (2020). *What Percentage of Small Businesses Fail? (And Other Need-to-Know Stats)*. Fundera. www.fundera.com/blog/what-percentage-of-small-businesses-fail

U.S. Department of Education. (2019, August 30). *A Guide to the Individualized Education Program*. U.S. Department of Education. https://www2. ed.gov/parents/needs/speced/iepguide/index.html

U.S. Small Business Administration. (n.d.). *Write Your Business Plan*. U.S. Small Business Administration. www.sba.gov/business-guide/plan-your-business/write-your-business-plan

3

Launching Your Educational Consulting Business

John Sowash is an international speaker, educational technology consultant and CEO of Sowash Ventures, a company he started in 2011. Here is the plain, yet pivotal advice he received from his mentor when he was just getting started as an entrepreneur:

"Stop talking about it. Stop thinking about it. Do it!"

John elaborated: "It is better, in my opinion, to figure it out along the way, than to pretend that you can actually figure it all out before you start."

When to Start Your Business

How do you know when it is time to launch your educational consulting business? You don't. You just do it! If you are reading this book, then that is a clear sign you may be ready to move forward. Preparation is appropriate and helpful, which is why building a business plan is delineated in the previous chapter. No matter where you are in the business planning process, there is no cause for you to hesitate to launch your consultancy. You can start today. Nevertheless, there is one glaringly obvious reason why you may not be ready to proceed: you're afraid. Starting a business is scary!

DOI: 10.4324/9781003172307-3

Put Fear in the Back Seat

In her 2015 New York Times bestselling book, "Big Magic: Creative Living Beyond Fear," Elizabeth Gilbert writes a "welcoming speech" to fear that she delivers before she takes on any new endeavor:

> Dearest Fear: Creativity and I are about to go on a road trip together. I understand you'll be joining us, because you always do. I acknowledge that you believe you have an important job to do in my life, and that you take your job seriously. Apparently your job is to induce complete panic whenever I'm about to do anything interesting – and, may I say, you are superb at your job. So by all means, keep doing your job, if you feel you must. But I will also be doing my job on this road trip, which is to work hard and stay focused. And Creativity will be doing its job, which is to remain stimulating and inspiring. There's plenty of room in this vehicle for all of us, so make yourself at home, but understand this: Creativity and I are the only ones who will be making any decisions along the way. I recognize and respect that you are part of this family, and so I will never exclude you from our activities, but still – your suggestions will never be followed. You're allowed to have a seat, and you're allowed to have a voice, but you are not allowed to have a vote. You're not allowed to touch the road maps; you're not allowed to suggest detours; you're not allowed to fiddle with the temperature. Dude, you're not even allowed to touch the radio. But above all else, my dear old familiar friend, you are absolutely forbidden to drive.
>
> (Gilbert, 2015, 25–26)

In her "welcoming speech," Gilbert makes it clear that she is not trying to tell fear to "go away," rather, she invites it along for the ride. Similarly, it is unrealistic to expect that you can suppress or ignore your fears about starting your business. The key to this story is that fear may be in the car, but it is not in the driver's seat.

Tackle Fear by Talking About It – With the Right Person

One of the easiest ways to tackle fear is by talking about it. It is important, however, for you to practice discernment when sharing your fears about your business, especially in the early phases of its development. Do not expect "Debbie Downer" or "Gloomy Gus" to suddenly perk up when you tell them that you are planning to take the risky step of starting your own business. You know which of your friends and colleagues are equipped to handle your delicate trepidations with care. It may not be time to talk to certain family members, either. Parents, siblings, and other trusted relatives may have your best interest at heart, but often do not have the expertise or experience to give an informed opinion about what you are trying to establish.

Private fears, left unchecked, are unbound by rational considerations or even simple logic. In your mind's eye, potential clients may laugh in your face, or you may even be exposed to your peers as an ignoramus who knows nothing about your purported area of expertise. You may envision your business failing in spectacular fashion! But, if you talk to either someone who supports and understands your entrepreneurial vision or a mental health professional, it is very unlikely that they will affirm your nightmarish imaginings. Instead, they can provide much-needed encouragement, constructive feedback, and help you strategize in ways that will assuage even your most unsettling misgivings. Remember, you are not in this alone. There are many people who would be happy to help you make your dreams come true.

The Biggest Fear of All: Imposter Syndrome

According to Kirsten Weir in her American Psychological Association web article, "Feel like a fraud?":

> First described by psychologists Suzanne Imes, PhD, and Pauline Rose Clance, PhD, in the 1970s, impostor phenomenon [i.e. impostor syndrome], occurs among high achievers who are unable to internalize and accept their success. They often attribute their accomplishments to luck rather than to ability, and fear that others will eventually unmask them as a fraud . . . The impostor phenomenon seems to be more common among people who are embarking on a new endeavor, says Imes.
>
> (Weir, 2013)

New educational consultants may be particularly susceptible to this. Many of them enter the field, in part, because of their myriad professional achievements and recognition for exceptional work as educators and school leaders. Additionally, starting a business is the epitome of "embarking on a new endeavor." Impostor syndrome can paralyze even the most sought-after, knowledgeable and capable individual and impede them from pursuing even the smallest first step towards capitalizing on their own expertise.

In the same article, Weir offers a list of ways to "overcome the belief that you don't measure up":

- ◆ Talk to your mentors
- ◆ Recognize your expertise
- ◆ Remember what you do well
- ◆ Realize no one is perfect
- ◆ Change your thinking
- ◆ Talk to someone who can help

(Weir, 2013)

You cannot allow imposter syndrome to rob you of the opportunity to chase your dream. If you are a practicing or former educator, your students and their families have certainly benefited from your know-how. You probably have been recognized by your peers, subordinates, and supervisors for the high quality of your work. Some of your close friends and family members may have even expressed their confidence in your professional ability. The belief that you do not know what you're doing or that you will be exposed as a charlatan is simply an illusion fueled by self-doubt. People believe in you and your talent. You are competent. You made it this far because of your unique skills and experience. You have what it takes to make your business successful.

Block Fear by Being Intentional

Another way to obstruct fear is to be intentional about designing your business in ways that directly address the concerns that you are still holding onto. This doesn't mean that you are letting fear into the driver's seat. It means that you are answering fear's questions, so it can relax and let you and creativity get your work done in peace! While it is not okay to let fear drive your decision-making, it can help you identify specific areas in which you may need to do some extra planning or solicit help from others. Whatever you are afraid of, do not avoid it. Be intentional about facing your fears head on and transform what are now obstacles into advantages for you and your business.

For example, if your fear is that you will not be able to properly manage the money that your business generates, then be intentional about facing this concern. Track your business income and expenses carefully. Consult with an accountant experienced with small businesses to get help with setting up your financial systems. Build an ideal budget based on your projected income for the next year. Then, create a few contingency budgets in which you decide how to cut operational costs and/or generate income from alternative sources in the (likely) event that you do not bring in as much business income as you projected in your original, ideal budget.

Public speaking anxiety, or glossophobia, affects about 73% of the U.S. population (Montopoli, 2017). This particular fear may be an impediment to readers of this book, as speaking to large groups of teachers, administrators, or other stakeholders is often a significant aspect of educational consulting. Fortunately, there are many resources and support groups available for people who suffer from this very common phobia. Joining a public-speaking group like your local chapter of Toastmasters, or working with a therapist or psychologist to find interventions and therapies to help alleviate this fear can also be helpful.

 ## Do Now: What Are You Afraid Of?

List reasons why you are not ready to start your business or the fears you have about your current business. Discuss these fears with a trusted, supportive colleague and/or with a mental health professional. Ask for help with devising strategies to directly address and alleviate your fears.

Extra Credit: Revisit Your Business Plan

Go back to your business plan and make edits to prioritize tasks and goals that will help assuage any lingering concerns you have about your business. Updating your business plan in this way will help you to move forward unencumbered by apprehension and uncertainty.

Four Ways to Start Your Business TODAY

Here is a (partial) list of ways to begin working as an independent educational consultant:

1 Serve as an intern or apprentice

Do you personally know someone who has recently launched an educational consulting business? If so, take advantage of the opportunity to help them enhance their consultancy, and at the same time, get a front row seat to the inner workings of an entrepreneurial endeavor similar to what you intend to build. Ask them if they would take you on as an intern and/or apprentice. Be prepared to volunteer your time and expertise or to offer it at a reduced cost, as you want to be of service to your fellow small businessperson. What you learn may be far more valuable than what you may earn if you charged your normal rate. Providing this much-needed help to a friend or colleague will surely position you to get the assistance you need when you launch your business independently. As their consultancy grows, they may even ask you to take on paying clients that they are too busy to serve!

2 Work as a subcontractor

Want to start generating income as an independent educational consultant right away? Find companies and organizations that will contract you for your services. Keep in mind that this "middle-man" will charge clients at least twice and up to five times as much as they will pay you as a subcontractor. Nevertheless, while you may not yet make as much as you want to on individual jobs, large companies with lots of clients can quickly offer you a steady stream of bookings and income to help you more efficiently launch your business. For example, the author and several of the successful consultants quoted in this book have worked as national presenters for the Bureau of Education & Research (BER, https://ber.org/) who, according to their website, "is the leading provider of professional development and PD training resources for teachers and other educators in North America." Through companies like BER, fledgling consultants can receive much needed compensation, exposure, and support from fellow subcontractors and company leadership.

3 Present at a conference

Research the professional organizations affiliated with your field of expertise and apply to present at their conferences. If you are just getting started, you may want to look at local and regional events first, as they are much more likely to accept your presentation proposals. As you gain more experience, you may be selected to share your knowledge at national and international meetings. Although these opportunities are often unpaid, you may also receive a discount or even a waiver on the event's registration fee. Eventually, you can get paid to do keynote addresses and extended workshops. Even if you are not a presenter, make it a point to attend at least a few conferences each year to enhance your professional knowledge and to connect with presenters and other attendees. Presenting at and attending conferences expose you to a broader audience to whom you can market your services. Conferences are great places to engage with thought leaders in your field and make valuable associations with new colleagues and clients.

Tech Tip: Participate in an Online Conference

Online conferences present unique, convenient opportunities to network with individuals who you would not normally meet at an in-person gathering. Since these meetings are much less expensive to produce, they are often free or offered at a reduced cost to participants. If you are working full-time, you can find international events that occur in a different time zone, allowing for you to participate late at night or early in the morning and meet new colleagues from all over the world. Organizations that present live conferences often supplement their offerings with online events for remote attendees. Search the internet to find out more information.

4 Offer your services to your current employer

If you are working in a school, district, or another educational entity, it is likely that what you plan to do as a consultant could be utilized in your present position. Arrange a meeting with your supervisor in which you offer to provide whatever services you want to hone for your consultancy. For instance, if teacher training will be your business's primary offering, then submit a request to start conducting professional development sessions for the teachers in your workplace that directly address institutional needs and priorities, and tap into your specific skill set. You may be able to negotiate supplemental compensation for your additional labor. Not only could this be a source of extra income, but it will also give you valuable experience as you transition to doing your work independently.

When/How/If to Quit Your "Day Job"

Many of the educational consultants interviewed for this book reported that they started their businesses while they were still working as full-time teachers, administrators, or other school and/or district-based positions. In

Start Educational Consulting Today

Serve as an intern or apprentice

You'll be better positioned to launch your own business, and may even receive referrals.

Work as a subcontractor

Although the "middle man" takes a cut, you'll earn compensation, exposure, and support from fellow sub-contractors.

Present at a conference

You'll reach a broad audience and make valuable associations with new colleagues and clients.

Offer your services to your current employer

You may be able to negotiate additional compensation, and can gain experience within your current workplace.

fact, several of them are still working full-time in addition to working inde-pendently as educational consultants. As is discussed in Chapter 1, "Begin with your WHY," quitting your day job is not a valid reason to start a busi-ness. It may be a goal or milestone that you hope to achieve, or not. Many successful consultants never quit their day job, but still build strong repu-tations and followings through their independent work. Edtech consultant, presenter, attorney, author, teacher, and founder of THRIVEinedu LLC Con-sulting, Rachelle Dene Poth, describes herself as a "full-time teacher and full-time consultant."

Some educators find more fulfillment in knowing that they not only established a successful business, but they grew it to a point where they were able to be full-time businesspeople. Another attractive path involves expanding your business to employ and empower other educational con-sultants. Former high school English teacher, Mark Wagner, is a founder and former CEO of EdTechTeam, an international educational technology consultancy, which at the height of its popularity, offered over 100 confer-ences, provided training for over 50,000 teachers, and hired over 400 con-tractors, each year, many of whom were educational consultants. He said: "One thing I always felt good about is that we helped a lot of teachers share their expertise, help other teachers and bring more [money] home at the end of the year."

When thinking about this topic, do not limit your considerations to finances. If your spouse or partner is willing to support you financially, or if you have a nest egg you can pull from, you may be able to build your busi-ness without worrying about an initial period of little to no income. Money can always be made, but time is irreplaceable. Really evaluate your schedule and if you are willing to put in the extra time it takes to establish a consul-tancy. You may decide to quit your job or work part-time to reduce stress. There is no magic formula one can use to calculate when or if the time is perfectly right to transition into full-time entrepreneurship. You have to think deeply about your own circumstances, what matters to you and your family, and whether the conditions are right (or ever will be) for you to quit your "day job."

☑ Check for Understanding: Calling It a "Side Hustle"

Would you be thrilled to learn that the hairdresser you are trusting to give you a new, dramatic haircut was just doing hair "on the side"? Would you want your pharmacist to tell you that they cannot fill your prescription because that's not their "day job"? Of course not. Even if you choose to keep your "day job," never refer to your business as a "side hustle." In 2014, the late Dr. Maya Angelou said:

> Words are things. . . . Someday we'll be able to measure the power of words. I think they are things. They get on the walls. They get in your wallpaper. They get in your rugs, in your upholstery, and your clothes, and finally into you.
>
> (Oprah Winfrey Network, 2014)

Accordingly, the words you use to describe your consultancy matter. Even if you do not explicitly communicate to clients and other stakeholders that you view your consultancy as a "side hustle," this perception will come through in the way that you do business.

Your clients deserve high-quality work, and your success depends on it. Rather than embracing the "side hustle" label, plan to manage your business's growth in ways that account for the fact that your time is limited without compromising the level of customer service you provide for patrons. For example, many consultants employ part-time assistants to manage their calendar and client communication. You may hire subcontractors to take on engagements for which you are unavailable. More information on hiring help will be provided in Chapter 8, "How and Why to Grow Your Business." It is okay to keep your "day job." It is not okay to diminish the significance of your entrepreneurial endeavors by relegating them to the dubious category of a "side hustle."

Exit Ticket: Next Steps

What can you do within the next 30 days to launch your educational consulting business? Who do you need to talk to? What steps do you need to take? Write 3–5 steps down (keep it doable) and begin working on them immediately.

Chapter Review: You Can Start Small, But You Must START

In his book, "Start: Punch Fear in the Face, Escape Average and Do Work That Matters," Jon Acuff writes:

> If you want help for your dream, start by helping someone else with their dream. If you want support for your hope, start by giving

support to someone else's hope. If you want encouragement as you work on your calling, start by encouraging other people. Giving support is often the best way to get it.

(Acuff, 2013)

The easiest way to launch your business is to connect with and assist individuals, groups, and organizations who are already working in the specific area you are interested in or have needs that correlate with the services you want to provide. You can always start small, but in order to build your business into everything you dreamed of, you must start.

Reference List

Acuff, J. (2013). *Start*. Ramsey Press.

Gilbert, E. (2015). *Big Magic: Creative Living Beyond Fear*. Riverhead Books.

Montopoli, J. (2017, February 20). *Public Speaking Anxiety and Fear of Brain Freezes*. National Social Anxiety Center. https://nationalsocialanxiety-center.com/2017/02/20/public-speaking-and-fear-of-brain-freezes

Oprah Winfrey Network. (2014). *Dr. Maya Angelou on the Power of Words* [Video]. YouTube. www.youtube.com/watch?v=BKv65MdlV-c

Weir, K. (2013, November). *Feel Like a Fraud?* American Psychological Association. www.apa.org/gradpsych/2013/11/fraud

4

Establishing Your Business
(Paperwork + Incorporation)

Eboni Walker, founder of Learning Matters Early Childhood Consulting, has cultivated a broad background in early childhood education, research, and educational policy for almost 20 years. She has taught children from preschool through first grade and has worked as a trainer and research analyst for the Office of Head Start and the U.S. Department of Education. On the topic of establishing your business with proper paperwork and other required processes, she shared:

> Going about the process of registering with the state, filling out the paperwork and getting an LLC organized – I did that right away. It took me the first one or two months to set that up properly. It was important, because then I could . . . position myself as a vendor with different organizations, [as] I was certified, on the books, as a business.

In this chapter, you will learn all about what you must do to be recognized as a legitimate business by your stakeholders, the state you live in, and the Internal Revenue Service. It can as simple as answering the following seven questions:

1   What is your business's name?
2   How will your business be structured?
3   Where is your business located?
4   What is your business's phone number?
5   How can your business be found on the internet?
6   What is your Employer Identification Number (EIN)?
7   Are you registered with your state?

DOI: 10.4324/9781003172307-4

7 Steps to Establish Your Business

1 What is your business name?

2 How will your business be structured?

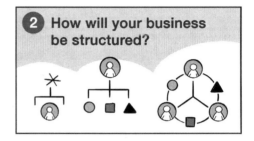

3 Where is your business located?

4 How can your business be found on the Internet?

5 What is your business phone number?

6 What is your Employer Identification Number (EIN)?

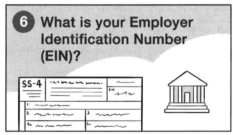

7 Are you registered with your state?

What Is Your Business's Name?

The first major decision that must be made before you can go about legally establishing your business is what you and your stakeholders will call your establishment. The importance of this step cannot be overstated. Everything you do moving forward, from registering with your state and the Internal Revenue Service (IRS), to branding and marketing your business will hinge on this critical choice. Therefore, this is a step that you should take VERY seriously. Do not be hasty. It is not easy to change your business name, as it will require updating with several entities, including your state government and the IRS, and possibly overhauling your branding and marketing to promote your new label.

Many consultants use their own name in some form as their business name. For example, the author's consulting business is called "Tinashe Blanchet and Associates." This can prove advantageous when your goal is to market yourself and make your name well-known in your industry. Michael Zipursky, CEO and co-founder of Consulting Success, writes:

> Using your name as a business name makes sense if you are the brand. If your consulting business is very personal, and buyers are reaching out to and buying from you because they see you as the expert, then it's a good idea to name your firm after yourself.
>
> (Zipursky, 2015)

Educational consultants definitely fit this description, as schools and organizations work with these individuals based on their personal brand and expertise.

If you are not yet sure about what to call your establishment, don't let this be a reason for you not to proceed with starting your business. Until you decide, you can do work independently as an individual, or an unregistered sole proprietorship, using your social security number (SSN) for tax identification. Some educational consultants choose to do business only in this way and claim all their business income on their personal taxes. There is not that much to it; just use your own name and SSN when filling out client paperwork. While this is a viable path to working independently, it will not protect you from liability to clients, subcontractors, and/or other stakeholders. Accordingly, this chapter will provide all the information you need to establish your consultancy as a separate entity from yourself, with its own identification number that will be independent of you for primarily legal and taxation purposes. The vast majority of the consultants interviewed for this book agree that this is the best way to set up your business for long-term stability, solvency, and growth.

✓ Check for Understanding: Using Your Own Name

There are many reasons to title your business more broadly than simply using your own name. The author, who used her married name for her business, is now divorced and could remarry and take her new husband's last name. This can have serious repercussions for her business. In his article, "How to Choose a Consulting Firm Name," Zipursky asks:

> Do [you] want to create a consulting business that is much larger than you? Do you envision a time where there are going to be other consultants or employees working at your firm? If so, naming the business after yourself might not be the best approach. If you want to build a bigger firm, then your name should convey more about what you do as a consulting firm. If the name is attached to you and you're planning to grow your consulting business with a potential to exit – to sell the business down the road – having that name directly attached to you isn't the best decision.
>
> (Zipursky, 2015)

 ## Do Now: Confirm the Availability of Your Name

Before you settle on a name for your business, make sure that it is available to be registered in your state. Visit your secretary of state's website (see Table 2.2 later in this chapter) and conduct a business entity search to make sure that the name you chose is available. You may need to tweak it slightly to make sure it is unique. For example, when the author launched a non-profit organization in 2014, she wanted to simply call it "The Learning Laboratory." When she tried to register this company in Louisiana, that name was already taken. Consequently, she adapted it and settled on "The Learning Laboratory New Orleans, Inc."

 ## Tech Tip: Do a Web Search for Your Name

Even if your proposed business name is available in your state, you may still want to change it, if it is commonly used. If your name is Michael Smith, then

"Michael Smith & Associates" is probably not the business name you want to utilize, as a quick web search for this name brings up over 91 million results! Take the time to search the web to see if your name is already in use. It is okay if your name is not unique on the internet. But, you may want to know how common it is and the nature of the other results that will appear when your business name is searched.

How Will Your Business Be Structured?

Another important decision for you to make is the legal structure under which you will organize and incorporate your business. Most of the consultants interviewed for this book set up their firms as limited liability companies (LLCs). In his article, "The Best Business Structures for Consultants," Jay Niblick offers three ways your business structure can impact how you operate your business:

1 **Ease of formation**: Starting a business can require a hefty amount of paperwork and other administrative duties, or none at all, depending on the legal entity you choose.
2 **Taxation**: Not all business structures are taxed equally. Being strategic in your choice of a legal entity may allow you to take home more in profits and pay less in taxes.
3 **Liability**: Certain business structures make you personally liable for failures of the business, which may mean you have to pay damages out of your own pocket, or through valuable assets like your house or car. Other entities provide more protection for you – and your personal assets – in the event of a lawsuit.

Among several different types of businesses that one can choose when incorporating in the United States, there are four structures that are most commonly used by consultants (Niblick, 2019). They are defined on the SBA website (www.sba.gov/business-guide/launch-your-business/choose-business-structure) as follows:

1 Sole proprietorship/Partnership

A sole proprietorship is easy to form and gives you complete control of your business. You're automatically considered to be a sole proprietorship if you do business activities but don't register as any other kind of business. Sole proprietorships do not produce a separate business entity. This means your business assets and liabilities are not separate from your personal assets and liabilities. You can be held personally liable for the debts and obligations of the business. Sole proprietors are still able to get a trade name. It can also be hard to raise money because you can't sell stock, and banks are hesitant to lend to sole proprietorships. Sole proprietorships can be a good choice for low-risk businesses and owners who want to test their business idea before forming a more formal business.

Partnerships are the simplest structure for two or more people to own a business together. There are two common kinds of partnerships: limited partnerships (LP) and limited liability partnerships (LLP). Limited partnerships have only one general partner with unlimited liability, and all other partners have limited liability. The partners with limited liability also tend to have limited control over the company, which is documented in a partnership agreement. Profits are passed through to personal tax returns, and the general partner – the partner without limited liability – must also pay self-employment taxes. Limited liability partnerships are similar to limited partnerships, but give limited liability to every owner. An LLP protects each partner from debts against the partnership, they won't be responsible for the actions of other partners. Partnerships can be a good choice for businesses with multiple owners, professional groups, and groups who want to test their business idea before forming a more formal business.

2 Limited liability company

An LLC lets you take advantage of the benefits of both the corporation and partnership business structures. LLCs protect you from personal liability in most instances, your personal assets – like your vehicle, house, and savings accounts – won't be at risk in case your LLC faces bankruptcy or lawsuits. Profits and losses can get passed through to your personal income without facing corporate taxes. However, members of an LLC are considered self-employed and must pay self-employment tax contributions towards Medicare and Social Security. LLCs can have a limited life in many states. When a member joins or leaves an LLC, some states may require the LLC to be dissolved and re-formed with new membership – unless there's already an agreement in place within the LLC for buying, selling, and transferring ownership. LLCs can be a good choice for medium- or higher-risk businesses, owners with significant personal assets they want to be protected, and owners who want to pay a lower tax rate than they would with a corporation.

3 S corp

An S corporation, sometimes called an S corp, is a special type of corporation that's designed to avoid the double taxation drawback of regular C corps. S corps allow profits, and some losses, to be passed through directly to owners' personal income without ever being subject to corporate tax rates. Not all states tax S corps equally, but most recognize them the same way the federal government does and taxes the shareholders accordingly. Some states tax S corps on profits above a specified limit and other states don't recognize the S corp election at all, simply treating the business as a C corp. S corps must file with the IRS to get S corp status, a different process from registering with their state. There are special limits on S corps. S corps can't have more than 100 shareholders, and all shareholders must be U.S. citizens. You'll still have to follow strict filing and operational processes of a C corp. S corps also have an independent life, just like C corps. If a shareholder leaves the company or sells his or her shares, the S corp can continue doing business relatively undisturbed. S corps can be a good choice for a businesses that would otherwise be a C corp, but meet the criteria to file as an S corp.

4 C corp

A corporation, sometimes called a C corp, is a legal entity that's separate from its owners. Corporations can make a profit, be taxed, and can be held legally liable.

Corporations offer the strongest protection to its owners from personal liability, but the cost to form a corporation is higher than other structures. Corporations also require more extensive record-keeping, operational processes, and reporting. Unlike sole proprietors, partnerships, and LLCs, corporations pay income tax on their profits. In some cases, corporate profits are taxed twice – first, when the company makes a profit, and again when dividends are paid to shareholders on their personal tax returns. Corporations have a completely independent life separate from its shareholders. If a shareholder leaves the company or sells his or her shares, the C corp can continue doing business relatively undisturbed. Corporations have an advantage when it comes to raising capital because they can raise funds through the sale of stock, which can also be a benefit in attracting employees. Corporations can be a good choice for medium- or higher-risk businesses, businesses that need to raise money, and businesses that plan to "go public" or eventually be sold.

(U.S. Small Business Administration, n.d.)

Niblick offers some additional guidance on choosing a structure for consultants:

When deciding between business entities, first ask yourself whether you want or need to incorporate as a consultant. Legally, you don't have to incorporate, and maybe that smaller degree of maintenance would suit your business well. Then, weigh the advantages and disadvantages of each entity and choose the one with the ease of formation, taxation, and legal protection you think you can benefit from most:

- Many consultants prefer to operate an LLC than be a sole proprietor or a corporation owner because these entities combine many of the advantages of the other two entities. If you run a small operation and want to protect your assets, this is likely the best legal structure for your consulting business.
- Sole proprietorships are by far the easiest form of business to set up – but offer the least legal protection.
- An S Corporation structure is likely only an option if your consulting business is relatively large, with several shareholders and multiple employees. Protections are similar to those of an LLC, but shareholders have more responsibilities.
- If working as a consultant, there is little reason to consider a C Corporation as an option. Businesses seeking this structure are usually large firms with many employees and many shareholders. Your consultant business would need to be extensive and complex for you to need to go this route.

While these four options are the main types of business structures that will apply to you, [other] structures are also available, but consultants don't typically use them. Understand that you have an array of options for your business when it comes to picking your structure; picking your business structure comes down to what works best for you.

(Niblick, 2019)

Table 4.1 Business Structure Comparison Chart

Structure	Ownership	Liability	Taxes
Sole proprietorship	One person	Unlimited personal liability	Personal tax only
Partnerships	Two or more people	Unlimited personal liability unless structured as a limited partnership	Self-employment tax (except for limited partners) Personal tax
Limited liability company (LLC)	One or more people	Owners are not personally liable	Self-employment tax Personal tax or corporate tax
Corporation – S corp	One or more people, but no more than 100, and all must be U.S. citizens	Owners are not personally liable	Personal tax
Corporation – C corp	One or more people	Owners are not personally liable	Corporate tax

Source: U.S. Small Business Administration (n.d.)

Where Is Your Business Located?

When you register your business with the state and the IRS, you will be asked for your address. Securing a PO Box is a great option if you want to set up a business mailing address that is separate from your residence. However, you will still need to provide a physical address in addition to your mailing address on your business filing paperwork. You may only have a home address for this purpose, and that is okay. This could be advantageous for tax purposes, as you will be able to claim part of your rent, mortgage, and utility costs as business expenses, offsetting your overall tax liability.

If you would like to have a workspace that is separate from your home, an affordable, attractive option is to utilize a coworking space, or a membership-based workspace where diverse groups of freelancers, remote workers, and other independent professionals work together in a shared, communal setting. Most of these spaces are accessible 24–7, offering independent workers a high level of flexibility around their operating schedule. Coworking spaces also offer valuable opportunities to connect and collaborate with other entrepreneurs. (Spreitzer et al., 2015, 1–5)

What Is Your Business's Phone Number?

While using your home address is fine, it is typically not advisable to use your personal phone number for your business. For instance, you do not want to answer your home or cell phone in an informal manner only to realize that you are speaking with a client or other business associate. There are many ways to secure a business phone. You can talk to your phone company about getting a second line or a business account. You can employ a professional answering service, live or automated, to field business calls. However you decide to do it, creating a separate phone line for your firm is an important step in forming your business as a legitimate, independent entity.

Tech Tip: Get a Business Phone Number for Free With Google Voice

Google Voice (voice.google.com) is a free service where you can create a unique phone number for your business to receive calls and SMS text messages. Although you will receive a separate number, it can be set up to ring to your cell phone. You can also make and receive calls, check voicemail and text messages on your computer at the Google Voice website or using the Google Voice app on your smartphone or tablet. By default, Google Voice screens calls and you will hear the name of the caller before you answer, ensuring that you are prepared to speak to a business contact. Google Voice has many valuable features for business owners, including automatic voicemail transcription. Call forwarding is also available, meaning you can have your assistant or another individual receive your business calls, and receive text messages and voicemail transcripts.

How Can Your Business Be Found on the Internet?

Establishing your business's web presence is equally, if not more, important than setting up your physical address and telephone number. Many potential clients, subcontractors, and other stakeholders will do an internet search for your business to learn more about your background and the services you offer. You can also include online forms on your site for individuals and organizations to contact you or inquire about your services. While there are many tools that you can use to create your own website, it may be more beneficial for you to secure the services of a web designer to build a polished, professional-looking web presence.

Additionally, social media platforms including Facebook, Twitter, and Instagram offer other ways to connect with stakeholders on the internet. Lastly, a key part of organizing business-related correspondence is to make an email address specifically for your consultancy. It is easy to create a free account using tools like Gmail, Hotmail, or Yahoo, but it is much more professional to have an email address at your own domain, i.e., "yourname@ yourbusiness.com." More information about how to build and utilize your business's website, create an email address and leverage social media will be discussed in Chapter 6, "Branding + Marketing."

Do Now: Research Websites and Social Media Profiles

Search the internet to find the websites and social media profiles of other successful educational consultants you know personally, or who you have heard about. Also, identify popular firms who are simply easy to find on the web with a generic search term like "educational consultant." Take note of the type of information that is included on these sites and profiles. When you see a particularly attractive website, scroll to the bottom of the page to find out who designed it or what publishing tool was used to create it. Record all of the information you find, as it will be very helpful when you are ready to build your business's web presence.

What Is Your Employer Identification Number (EIN)?

Once you have settled on a name and legal structure for your business, contact the IRS to get an Employer Identification Number (EIN). This number is a unique identifier for your business that you may need to register with your state, open a business bank account and get paid by clients through your business. According to the IRS website: "You may apply for an EIN online if your principal business is located in the United States or U.S. Territories. The person applying online must have a valid Taxpayer Identification Number (SSN, ITIN, EIN)." To complete your EIN application online, visit https:// sa.www4.irs.gov/modiein/individual. This is the IRS's preferred method for you to apply. You should receive your EIN immediately when you complete the online form. To mail in or preview the items requested on the EIN application you can view or download Form SS-4 at www.irs.gov/pub/irs-pdf/ fss4.pdf.

Are You Registered With Your State?

Typically, your Secretary of State is responsible for registering corporations, limited liability companies (LLCs), and partnerships; handling mergers and acquisitions; and processing the articles of dissolution in the event that you close down your business. To start a consultancy that will be classified as anything beyond a sole proprietorship, familiarize yourself with your state's regulations and tax filing requirements. In Table 2.2, you will find your state's Secretary of State website to learn more about certain filing requirements for where you live and phone numbers to call if you have specific questions. (Allen, 2021)

Table 4.2 Secretary of State Directory

State Office	Website	Phone #
Alabama Secretary of State	www.sos.state.al.us	334–242–7200
Alaska Lt. Governor	https://ltgov.alaska.gov	907–269–7460
Arizona Secretary of State	www.azsos.gov	602–542–4285
Arkansas Secretary of State	www.sosweb.state.ar.us	501–682–1010
California Secretary of State	www.sos.ca.gov	916–653–7244
Colorado Secretary of State	www.sos.state.co.us	303–894–2200
Connecticut Secretary of State	https://portal.ct.gov/sots	860–509–6200
Delaware Secretary of State	www.state.de.us/sos	302–577–8161
DC Secretary of State	http://os.dc.gov	202–727–6306
Florida Secretary of State	www.dos.state.fl.us	850–245–6500
Georgia Secretary of State	https://sos.ga.gov	470–312–2800
Guam Government Site	www.guam.gov	671–475–9380
Hawaii Lt. Governor	www.hawaii.gov/ltgov	808–586–0255
Idaho Secretary of State	www.sos.idaho.gov	208–334–2300
Illinois Secretary of State	www.cyberdriveillinois.com	217–782–2201
Indiana Secretary of State	www.in.gov/sos	317–232–6536
Iowa Secretary of State	https://sos.iowa.gov	515–281–6230
Kansas Secretary of State	www.kssos.org	785–296–4564
Kentucky Secretary of State	www.sos.ky.gov	502–564–3490
Louisiana Secretary of State	www.sos.la.gov	225–922–2880
Maine Secretary of State	www.state.me.us/sos	207–626–8400
Maryland Secretary of State	www.sos.state.md.us	410–974–5521

State Office	Website	Phone #
Massachusetts Secretary of State	www.sec.state.ma.us	617–727–9180
Michigan Secretary of State	www.michigan.gov/sos	517–335–2436
Minnesota Secretary of State	www.sos.state.mn.us	651–201–1324
Mississippi Secretary of State	www.sos.ms.gov	601–359–1350
Missouri Secretary of State	www.sos.mo.gov	573–751–4936
Montana Secretary of State	http://sos.mt.gov	406–444–2034
Nebraska Secretary of State	www.sos.ne.gov	402–471–2554
Nevada Secretary of State	https://nvsos.gov	775–684–5708
New Hampshire Secretary of State	www.sos.nh.gov	603–271–3242
New Jersey Secretary of State	www.state.nj.us/state	609–777–2581
New Mexico Secretary of State	www.sos.state.nm.us	505–827–3600
New York Secretary of State	www.dos.ny.gov	518–486–9846
North Carolina Secretary of State	www.sosnc.gov	919–814–5400
North Dakota Secretary of State	https://sos.nd.gov	701–328–2900
Ohio Secretary of State	www.sos.state.oh.us	614–466–2655
Oklahoma Secretary of State	www.sos.ok.gov	405–521–3912
Oregon Secretary of State	https://sos.oregon.gov	503–986–1523
Pennsylvania Secretary of State	www.dos.pa.gov	717–787–6485
Puerto Rico Secretary of State	www.estado.pr.gov/es	787–722–2121
Rhode Island Secretary of State	www.sos.ri.gov	401–222–2357
South Carolina Secretary of State	https://sos.sc.gov	803–734–2170
South Dakota Secretary of State	https://sdsos.gov	605–773–3537
Tennessee Secretary of State	https://sos.tn.gov	615–741–2819
Texas Secretary of State	www.sos.state.tx.us	512–463–5770
Utah Lt. Governor	https://ltgovernor.utah.gov	801–538–1041
Vermont Secretary of State	https://sos.vermont.gov	802–828–2148
Virgin Islands Secretary of State	http://ltg.gov.vi	340–774–2991
Virginia Secretary of State	https://commonwealth.virginia.gov	804–786–2441
Washington Secretary of State	www.secstate.wa.gov	360–902–4151
West Virginia Secretary of State	www.wvsos.com	304–558–6000
Wisconsin Secretary of State	https://sos.wi.gov	608–266–8888
Wyoming Secretary of State	http://soswy.state.wy.us	307–777–7378

Source: Allen (2021)

The total cost to register your business will usually be less than $300, but fees vary depending on your state and business structure.

The information you will need to register typically includes:

- ◆ Business name
- ◆ Business location
- ◆ Ownership, management structure, or directors
- ◆ Registered agent information
- ◆ Number and value of shares (if you're a corporation)

The documents you will have to produce will vary based on your state and business structure: (U.S. Small Business Administration, n.d.)

Table 4.3 Required Documents by Business Structure

Structure	Document	Description
LLC	Articles of organization	Articles of organization is a simple document that describes the basics of your LLC. It includes business information like the company name, address, member names, and the registered agent.
	LLC operating agreement	An operating agreement describes the structure of your company's financial and functional decisions. It defines how key business decisions are made, as well as each member's duties, powers, and responsibilities. It's widely recommended to create one to protect yourself and your business, even if your state doesn't mandate it.
Limited partnership	Certificate of limited partnership	This simple document describes the basics of your limited partnership. It notifies the state of the partnership's existence and contains basic business information like the company name, address, and partner names. Not all states require it, and some states call it by a different name.
	Limited partnership agreement	A limited partnership agreement is an internally binding document between all partners that defines how business decisions get made, each partner's duties, powers, and responsibilities. It's widely recommended to create one to protect yourself and your business, even if your state doesn't mandate it.

Structure	Document	Description
Limited liability partnership	Certificate of limited liability partnership	This simple document describes the basics of your limited liability partnership. It notifies the state of the partnership's existence and contains basic business information like the company name, address, and partner names. Not all states require it, and some states call it by a different name.
	Limited liability partnership agreement	A limited liability partnership agreement is an internally binding document between all partners that defines how business decisions get made, each partner's duties, powers, and responsibilities. It's widely recommended to create one to protect yourself and your business, even if your state doesn't mandate it.
Corporation (any kind)	Articles of incorporation	The articles of incorporation – or a certificate of incorporation – is a comprehensive legal document that lays out the basic outline of your business. It's required by every state when you incorporate. The most common information included is the company name, business purpose, number of shares offered, value of shares, directors, and officers.
	Bylaws or resolutions	Bylaws (called resolutions for nonprofits) are the internal governance documents of a corporation. They define how key business decisions are made, as well as officer and shareholders' duties, powers, and responsibilities. It's widely recommended to create one to protect yourself and your business, even if your state doesn't mandate it.

Source: U.S. Small Business Administration (n.d.)

Exit Ticket: Seven Questions to Answer

This chapter is designed to help you affirmatively answer seven critical questions:

1   What is your business's name?
2   How will your business be structured?
3   Where is your business located?

4   What is your business's phone number?
5   How can your business be found on the internet?
6   What is your Employer Identification Number (EIN)?
7   Are you registered with your state?

Follow the steps presented in the preceding pages to succinctly answer each one of these questions and you will be well on your way to setting up your firm to be formally recognized by the government and by the individuals, organizations, and companies with whom you seek to do business.

Extra Credit: Consult With a Lawyer or Business Consultant

The information presented in this chapter, while detailed, is not comprehensive. Depending on how you decide to organize your consultancy and your state's unique legal requirements, there may be additional steps you need to take to make sure you are operating your business in accordance with state and federal law. You may want to hire an expert to assist you with filling your paperwork. Lawyers who specialize in business formation and incorporation and/or small business consultants can provide much-needed support and guidance in this regard.

Chapter Review: Don't Be Overwhelmed; Get Your Paperwork in Order

Of course, setting up your business legitimately can be an overwhelming proposition. There is a lot of ground for you to cover, and many choices for you to make. There is no set timeline for when all of your paperwork needs to be done. Some of the consultants interviewed for this book indicated that there are one or more aspects of their paperwork that is not yet complete. Nevertheless, this process does not have to take long, and it can really set you up for short- and long-term success.

Reference List

Allen, S. (2021, May 7). *Directory of Secretary of State Offices and Websites*. The Balance Small Business. www.thebalancesmb.com/secretary-of-state-websites-1201005

Niblick, J. (2019, November 19). *The Best Business Structures for Consultants*. The Balance Small Business. www.thebalancesmb.com/what-are-the-4-best-business-structures-for-consultants-845847

Spreitzer, G., Bacevice, P., and Garrett, L. (2015, September). Why People Thrive in Coworking Spaces. *Harvard Business Review*, 93(9), 1–6.

U.S. Small Business Administration. (n.d.). *Choose a Business Structure*. U.S. Small Business Administration. www.sba.gov/business-guide/launch-your-business/choose-business-structure

U.S. Small Business Administration. (n.d.). *Register Your Business*. U.S. Small Business Administration. www.sba.gov/business-guide/launch-your-business/register-your-business

Zipursky, M. (2015, October 9). *How to Choose a Consulting Firm Name*. Consulting Success. www.consultingsuccess.com/how-to-choose-a-consulting-firm-name

5

Making + Managing Your Money

Being an educational consultant can be very lucrative. Dr. Will Deyamport (nicknamed "Dr. Will") is an educator, digital transformation strategist, writer, and podcaster. In 2019, he released a film titled "The Edupreneur," that was featured by Forbes as a "documentary about teachers turning towards entrepreneurship" (Shulman, 2019). Dr. Will talked about how he felt when he received payment for his very first educational consulting gig:

> Did I just make $2,300 in seven hours, doing something that I do every day on my job? I'm thinking: this is almost as much money as I make in a month!

Like Dr. Will, many of the consultants interviewed for this book were pleasantly surprised when they learned just how much more money they would make as an independent contractor than as a school or district employee. In 2021, educational consultants made over $15,000 more per year than full-time teachers, according to Glassdoor (Glassdoor, 2021a, 2021b). Nevertheless, many interviewees also reported that making and managing money was an area in which they struggled significantly.

Specific tips and verbiage to insert into contracts and proposals will be included in this chapter. You will also find lots of practical advice in this chapter from consultants who deal with the ongoing challenge of making and managing the income they generate from their businesses.

DOI: 10.4324/9781003172307-5

Australia-based edtech consultant, Jim Sill of Deploy Learning, shared:

> I wish somebody would have told me about money and how to manage my taxes. We all get into consulting, I think, because we do good work and we're pretty confident that we can get business. But, how do I manage the money I'm bringing in? How do I manage Quick-Books? When do I hire an accountant? When do I hire a bookkeeper?

He continues:

> Then you do the work, and they send you that check, and you're like: "Woo-hoo! I can't believe that just happened." Then, you have to start going: "Well, how much of that do I get to pay myself, and how much do I leave in my company . . . because, you can't give yourself that whole check."

You Can't Give Yourself That Whole Check

Something the author learned, the hard way, is what Jim shared in no uncertain terms: "you can't give yourself that whole check." This unambiguous admonition has many implications for how you must set up and run your business. When you work for a school or district, the check that you receive every two weeks or each month does not represent your full salary. There are many items that are deducted from each payout, including, but not limited to: state and federal income taxes, social security tax, disability and life insurance, health insurance, and retirement costs. The moment you become an entrepreneur, you are now responsible for paying some or all of these expenses on your own. Additionally, your consultancy will have its own operational costs that you would not incur as an employee, such as phone and internet services, branding and marketing costs, and hired help, including accountants, lawyers, personal assistants, and more.

Unlike full time employment, which pays out on a predictable schedule, educational consulting work is not consistent. You may have periods of time where you are very busy, including the summer and "back to school" months when schools and districts are purchasing a lot of teacher training, keynote speeches, and other services in preparation for the new school year. There will also be times when you may not get as much work, like spring testing. You must remember that comparing your pay as a full-time employee to what you can make as an independent contractor is like comparing apples to oranges; it is just not the same. Therefore, it is inappropriate for you to charge a rate that is solely based on what you would make in a full-time position.

What to Charge for Your Services

In his web article, "How much should I charge as a consultant?" Nathan Chan writes:

> If you have absolutely no idea where to start when setting consultation fees, take a look at your life. What are your personal expenses? What are your business expenses? What kind of lifestyle do you want to build or maintain as an independent consultant? Answering these questions will help you set a minimum price – a foundation upon which you can build your consulting fees.
>
> (Chan, 2020)

One of the best things about running your own business is that you get to make your own rules. So, it makes sense that you should begin thinking about what to charge based on how much you would like to make. If you still have a full-time job, what would make the extra effort to do consulting work in addition to your existing responsibilities worthwhile? If you are a full-time entrepreneur, how much do you want your yearly salary to be? How does this amount break down monthly, weekly, and for each individual gig? Asking yourself these specific questions will help you to get a clear idea as to how much you would like to charge.

 ## Do Now: Conduct Market Research

Once you are clear about how much you would like to make, you must do some research to find out what the market can bear. Pricing yourself too high will motivate potential clients to find someone else to do the same service for a lower rate. Pricing yourself too low can devalue your services. You do not want to be viewed as a "bargain-basement" consultant! Your rates should be somewhat consistent with what others charge for the same services, but also reflective of your unique experience and skill-set and your desired level of compensation. Conduct an online search to learn more about the amount consultants charge for the services you want to provide. This will yield limited results, as fees are often unpublished, so you may also want to talk to friends and colleagues who are already doing the work and are willing to share their rates with you.

Collecting Deposits and Setting Up Late Fees

Charging a non-refundable deposit is a way to ensure that individuals and entities who contract your services cannot cancel or change the terms of your agreement without penalty. This is particularly relevant when you conduct synchronous training or speaking engagements. Additionally, if you are expected to deliver services on location, then a deposit can pay or, at least, offset travel costs. Unfortunately, some schools and districts have financial regulations that may preclude them from making any form of prepayment. In these cases, you may request a purchase order (PO), which is a binding document in which your client agrees to pay your fee at a certain time. In the absence of a deposit or at least a PO, it would be unwise for a consultant to guarantee dates or deliverables.

Keep in mind that paying you for your services is probably one of very many items on your customer's to-do list. If there is no penalty for late payment, then compensating you in a timely manner may not be a priority. In most cases, it is not that clients are trying to "stiff" you, but there are other issues that can delay payment. For example, many districts require school board approval for expenditures over a certain amount. This and other bureaucratic processes can slow down the generation of your check. The purpose of your setting a late fee is not to collect extra payment, but to ensure that you will be paid on-time. Late fees or additional financial penalties are a great way to motivate individuals to cut through the "red tape" to head off any administrative issues that may slow down your remittance.

In Table 5.1, you will find contractual clauses used by the author to establish expectations for deposits and late payments.

When You Make the Rules, You Can Always Change Them

The author began collecting deposits and setting up late fees in response to a few difficult, yet enlightening experiences. To cite an instance, she once traveled across the country to conduct a full-day teacher training. The contract for this engagement articulated neither a deposit, nor a late fee, but the client assured her and her assistant that she would be paid on the date of her arrival. Against her better judgement, the author spent her own money to travel to the location and deliver the training. When she went to the school office to collect her payment, she was made to wait for over 30 minutes to be told that her check was not ready. The author had already incurred significant travel costs to get there, performed services for no compensation, and had to follow up for weeks to finally receive payment that was promised to be sent "as soon as possible."

Table 5.1 Deposit and Late Payment Contractual Verbiage

Deposit
A deposit of [50% of total stipend] is required in order to confirm the booking. The remaining balance will be due 48 business hours prior to the event. In the event of cancellation, (TRAINER) will re-book the program on a mutually convenient date with no penalty if the program is rescheduled within that calendar year. If the program is canceled and not rescheduled, the initial deposit will be considered full and complete payment. If the TRAINER attends the event and does not train due an error or discrepancy made by the CLIENT, CLIENT agrees to pay TRAINER for the full amount due.
Late Payment
If the TRAINER receives final payment after the due date above, the TRAINER may impose a late fee of $100.00. If the TRAINER receives payment from the CLIENT more than 30 days after the invoice date, the TRAINER may assess interest equal to five percent of the unpaid balance for each month, or a portion of the month the balance is unpaid. Interest accrues retroactively from the due date. If the CLIENT has not paid an invoice for more than 90 days, the TRAINER may refer collection of the unpaid amount to an attorney or collections agency. If the CLIENT's unpaid invoices are referred to an attorney or collections agency, the CLIENT shall pay all reasonable attorney's fees or collections agency fees in addition to the late fee and accrued interest.

While these types of situations do not happen often, when they do, you must ask yourself how you can better communicate expectations to prevent the same thing from happening again. Be flexible. As you work, you will want to add language to your contracts and proposals to protect you from repeating negative interactions and to more directly communicate your "rules of engagement." All of this can be developed over time and perhaps with the help of a legal expert who specializes in writing contracts.

While you will want to maintain some level of consistency in pricing across customers, you are not obligated to keep your prices the same for any extended period of time. You will not know exactly what to charge your patrons until you begin working independently. Part of figuring out your rates will depend on how people react to your pricing. For example, if you quote a prospective client a certain fee, and they immediately agree to it without hesitation, then that may be a clue that you probably could have charged at least a little bit more. Conversely, if you find that clients are consistently balking at your rates or not following through to book after receiving a quote, then that may indicate that you are charging too much.

Whatever you decide your initial rate is, understand that it will probably change as you continue to grow your customer base. This is especially true when you are in the earliest phases of your consultancy. For this reason, do not publish your rates online or otherwise. It is not about secrecy; it is about making sure that you maintain the flexibility to set pricing for each individual engagement. You make the rules when it comes to how much you charge and how you expect to be paid. Thus, you can always adjust them to meet your ever-changing needs.

⊘ Check for Understanding: Charging "By the Hour"

When you quote an expected payment for your services, bid an overall price based on completed deliverables, instead of the time spent. In Table 5.2, you will find language the author used in a proposal for consulting services to convey that she prefers not to work "by the hour." This verbiage was included in a sample proposal template written by Dr. Alan Weiss, an entrepreneurial coach, consultant, and speaker. The author included this note in many of her proposals and contracts, because it not only protected her from being "on the clock," but it also presented this expectation to patrons as a value proposition.

An hourly rate provides your clients with a compelling reason to focus not on the quality or the outcomes of your work, but rather on how much time it will take for you to complete it. As soon as you offer an hourly rate in a conversation about your compensation, inevitably, the question you will be asked next is: "how long should it take?" This is a very loaded question that you are probably unable to answer in an informed manner before actually doing the work.

John Sowash offered some additional feedback on the topic of "selling your time": "You are not selling your time. You are selling a solution. I try to price my services based on the value of the solution that I can provide. Now, this does sometimes result in some interesting conversations . . .

> **The client**: 'That only took you two hours to do!'
> **Me**: 'Yeah. It took me two hours . . . and ten years.'
> You're [also] paying for the years of experience that I provide to you!"

Table 5.2 Sample Contract/Proposal Language to Avoid Hourly Work

Terms and Conditions
My fees are always based upon the project, and never upon time units. That way you're encouraged to call upon me without worrying about a meter running, and I'm free to suggest additional areas of focus without concern about increasing your investment.

Source: Weiss (n.d.)

Hourly labor also exposes you to unrealistic or oppressive client expectations. You may be asked to rush your schedule in order to minimize or reduce costs. You may also be required to produce a detailed account of the specific dates and times during which you worked on an assigned project. In the unforgettable words of YouTube star Sweet Brown: "Ain't nobody got time for that!" (KFOR Oklahoma's News 4, 2012)

If you do choose to charge an hourly rate, at least make sure that the time for which you get paid includes preparation and research. Dr. John Staley, author, speaker, and Baltimore County Public Schools Coordinator of Special Projects, shared this relevant advice:

> If you're doing a workshop presentation, you just don't show up and it happens. You have to prepare for it. So all of that prep time – the time you take away from family, friends, relatives and whatever you want to do, you have to think about that. . . . So don't sell yourself cheap . . . know what your worth is.

Do Now: What Is Your Fee Structure?

Make a list of each of the individual services you would like to provide and the fees you plan to charge for each. Be specific. If you offer a full-day training, how many hours would you like to work, with lunch and other breaks? How does the price differ between in-person and virtual events? Remember to price not only for an engagement, but also for the research and preparation that goes into it. Do not forget to include travel costs for site visits. This is for your reference only. Do not share this document with clients, as you want to be flexible and responsive in your pricing.

Extra Credit: Determine Your Deposit and Late Fee Structure

Decide how much you like to be paid up front to turn away other inquiries about working on a certain date or to begin working on a project. This deposit amount should be a percentage, up to 50% of your total stipend. Late fees can be a flat rate, or a percentage, or both. This can be tricky. You want these fees to be high enough to deter clients from breaking your contract, but low enough as to not prevent clients from signing your contract in the first place. Of course, you can always adjust these amounts as you gain more experience.

Opening Your Business Bank Account

According to the SBA:

> As soon as you start accepting or spending money as your business, you should open a business bank account. Common business accounts include a checking account, savings account, credit card account, and a merchant services account. Merchant services accounts allow you to accept credit and debit card transactions from your customers." Most banks will request at least your EIN or SSN, if you're a sole proprietorship, and your business's formation documents. Be prepared for your bank of choice to ask for more information.
>
> (U.S. Small Business Administration, n.d.)

The SBA offers some great additional guidance on this topic:

Most business bank accounts offer perks that don't come with a standard personal bank account:

- ◆ **Protection**. Business banking offers limited personal liability protection by keeping your business funds separate from your personal funds. Merchant services also offer purchase protection for your customers and ensure that their personal information is secure.
- ◆ **Professionalism**. Customers will be able to pay you with credit cards and make checks out to your business instead of directly to you. Plus, you'll be able to authorize employees to handle day-to-day banking tasks on behalf of the business.
- ◆ **Preparedness**. Business banking usually comes with the option for a line of credit for the company. This can be used in the event of an emergency, or if your business needs new equipment.
- ◆ **Purchasing power**. Credit card accounts can help your business make large startup purchases and help establish a credit history for your business.

Some business owners open a business account at the same bank they use for their personal accounts. Rates, fees, and options vary from bank to bank, so you should shop around to make sure you find the lowest fees and the best benefits. Here are things to consider when you're opening a business checking or savings account:

- ◆ Introductory offers
- ◆ Interest rates for savings and checking
- ◆ Interest rates for lines of credit
- ◆ Transaction fees
- ◆ Early termination fees
- ◆ Minimum account balance fees

(U.S. Small Business Administration, n.d.)

Collecting Payments: The More, the Merrier

Most schools and districts will send you a check in the mail or give you a check in person at some point after services are rendered. But, when was the last time you wrote a check at the grocery store? Exchanging tangible funds, i.e., cash or check, through person-to-person transactions, is quickly becoming a relic of the past. Customers can now purchase goods and services independently online, and even in-person, through self-checkout, without interacting with a cashier or vendor. Credit and debit cards, electronic funds transfer, and even touchless payment by smartphone provide modern businesses with the important ability to offer lots of ways to pay.

Once you have figured out how much to charge, you must decide how you want to accept payments from your clients. When it comes to collecting cash, remember the saying: "the more the merrier." Of course, the more payments you receive, the merrier you will be! But, that's not all. The more ways you offer clients to pay you, the better off your business will be. Some individuals and entities can pay you immediately with a company credit card. Is your business set up to accept credit card payments? If it is, you will find that certain clients will pay you much faster in this manner than they would if they had to "cut a check." If you secure an extended contract or provide recurring services, inquire about receiving periodic payments by direct deposit. This is another way to minimize the wait time from invoice to remittance.

 ## Tech Tip: Use an Online Payment Processing Company

The author has used payment processing companies including PayPal (paypal.com), Stripe (stripe.com), and Square (squareup.com) to invoice clients and collect credit card payments online. The SBA writes:

> Payment processing companies are an increasingly popular alternative to traditional merchant services accounts. . . . If you find a

payment processor that you like, remember that you [may] still need to connect it to a business checking account to receive payments.

(U.S. Small Business Administration, n.d.)

In her article, "Credit Card Processing Fees: The Complete Guide," Priyanka Prakash said:

There are three main types of fees that can be included in the entirety of credit card processing:

- **Transaction fees**: These are the fees that you'll pay per transaction you process with a credit card. Transaction fees are made up of the interchange rate, the assessment fee, and the payment processor markup.
- **Flat fees**: These are the fees that you'll pay for working with a payment gateway or merchant services provider – the cost, essentially, for using their service. You'll typically pay these fees on a monthly basis.
- **Incidental fees**: Incidental fees are fees that you're charged by your payment processor or merchant account provider as a result of particular occurrences – like in the case of a chargeback or non-sufficient funds.

(Prakash, 2020)

Before you set up an account, make sure you research and compare all of these types of fees for at least a few different payment processors. Setting up one of these services can be a real game-changer for your company, as these tools make it very easy for you to request and receive payments as you communicate with patrons online.

Taxes: Pay Now, or Pay Later, but You Will Pay

Independent consultants are not just responsible for state and income taxes. Sole proprietors, members of partnerships, and LLC members are also required to pay self-employment tax, which is 15.3% of the first $142,800 of income you receive, plus 2.9% of anything you earn over this threshold in 2021 (Internal Revenue Service, n.d.). The recommended amount that independent consultants should put aside for this and state and federal taxes is 25–30% of your income after deductions for business expenses including office supplies, home office maintenance costs, and travel expenses. (Pant, 2021)

The vast majority of consultants interviewed for this book reported that withholding part of their income consistently to account for taxes is an area that they struggled with. You may pay your taxes now, or you can pay them later, but you will pay. It is very easy to start spending your business income without regard for the fact that you incur tax liability every time you collect payment. However, if you don't have a sound strategy for how to allocate incoming funds towards your inevitable tax debt, then you are setting yourself up for a big disappointment at tax time.

Here are a few tips for you to remember regarding taxes:

◆ Try to put aside at least a quarter of what you earn as a consultant to pay taxes each year. This may not be possible with every payment you receive. Stay focused on this goal nevertheless. If you are unable to reserve at least 25% of a specific payment, plan to save more the next time you get paid.

◆ If you find that it is too difficult to consistently save a quarter of your earnings, reduce the portion. Try allocating 20% or even 10% of what you bring in for taxes. Something is better than nothing. Anything you can do to offset what you will have to pay in taxes will be well worth the effort.

◆ File your taxes on time each year. You may be tempted to wait to file because you are afraid of how much you will owe. This is a poor strategy that will almost certainly result in a higher tax bill that includes penalties for filing late.

◆ Find a highly recommended and/or well-researched accountant who specializes in helping small businesses to do your taxes. Although this may be costly, a good accountant can save you a lot of money with deductions and other tactics to minimize your tax liability.

Budgeting for Your Business

Like writing a business plan or incorporating your business, budgeting can be an overwhelming proposition for a new entrepreneur. If you have already started working without one, then you know firsthand that it is absolutely possible to manage your money without this structure in place. In a 2020 survey of 335 small business owners and managers, half of the respondents reported that they did not have a formal budget at all (Roddy, 2021). In Chapter 2 of this book, *Writing a Business Plan*, readers also learned that half of small businesses fail within the first five years (McIntyre, 2020). While the author found no evidence that these two statistics are directly correlated, you may recall the adage that was shared in the second chapter regarding business planning: "If you fail to plan, then you plan to fail." Like a business plan, a budget can help set your consultancy up for success and solvency in the long term.

In the aforementioned 2020 survey, only about one-third (35%) of participants who created a budget spent more than they budgeted. Perhaps this suggests that when businesses make a budget, they are more likely to follow it. (Roddy, 2021) As a fledgling consultant, budgeting can be as simple as asking yourself two questions:

1   How much money do I expect to make? (income)
2   How will I spend my money? (expenses)

Make a list of what you come up with and how much of your income you are willing to allocate for each expense. Do not forget to plan for setting aside about 25% of your income for taxes! You may also want to consult with an accountant or bookkeeper to help you structure a budget that fulfills your personal and business goals. There are myriad ways to create an effective plan for how you want to spend (and save) the money you make.

Exit Ticket: Start Budgeting With a Spreadsheet

Use a spreadsheet to allocate and track your income and expenses. There are free business budget templates available online in the Google Sheets Template Gallery (docs.google.com/spreadsheets/u/0/?ftv=1) and Microsoft Excel (templates.office.com/en-us/Business-expense-budget-TM04035489) to help you get started.

When you use this budget, remember to go back each month and reconcile your projected income and expenses with what they actually were, making adjustments as needed. Like your business plan, your budget will be a living document that should evolve with your business over time. This will make your budget more realistic and easier to follow.

Extra Credit: Learn More About Business Budget Software

At some point, you may realize that a spreadsheet does not have enough functionality to meet the needs of a growing business. As you begin to hire employees and subcontractors, file and pay taxes, and project future income, you may want to "level up" your budgeting. Many software tools are available for you to use to manage your money and plan for the future in more sophisticated ways than your spreadsheet. According to Fundera.com:

> Budget software is a specific program that small businesses use to manage, track, and forecast their business budget. Budget software should have strong reporting capabilities that allow you to generate and manage financial statements like cash flow reports and profit and loss statements. Similar to standard accounting software, business budgeting software can also come with additional features such as payroll processing or payroll services . . . Before you dive into your options, consider how pricing, user experience, accounting tools, and more will play into your decision-making process. Then take a look at these top options for business budget software.
>
> (Weisner, 2021)

In Table 5.3, you will find three different tools that were listed as the best budgeting software for small businesses in 2021.

Table 5.3 Comparison Chart of Best Business Budgeting Software

Software	Website	Pros(+)/Cons(-)	Minimum Cost
QuickBooks Best for overall functionality	quickbooks.intuit.com	+ Easy to navigate + Customizable reports + Multiple users + Can separate personal and business expenses – Can be pricey – May be difficult for non-finance professionals – Hard to set up	$25/month* *QuickBooks Self-Employed starts at $15/month
FreshBooks Best for basic budgeting	freshbooks.com	+ Easily integrates with other web services + Very easy to navigate + Sophisticated reporting + Simple invoice creation – Can get very expensive with higher plans/adding team members – Doesn't allow for complex budgeting	$15/month

Software	Website	Pros(+)/Cons(-)	Minimum Cost
Xero Best for advanced features	xero.com	+ Excellent integration capabilities + Relatively affordable + Accessible user interface + Strong customer service + Unlimited users – Limited reporting options – Not ideal for larger businesses	$9/month

Source: Weisner (2021)

Chapter Review: You Have to Pay the Cost to Be the Boss

Making your own rules when it comes to money is one of the best parts of being an entrepreneur. You are the boss. Being the boss means that you get to decide how you want to collect payments and the terms under which you are to be paid. It also means that you have to be very shrewd about how you spend the money you earn. As previously mentioned, you can't give yourself that whole check! You may often be tempted to go with the least expensive options for the goods and services your business needs, but you must be willing to spend a little more to get exactly what you envision for your consultancy. Not only do you need to plan for taxes and other necessary expenses, but you must be willing to invest in your business for it to thrive and grow.

Reference List

Chan, N. (2020, July 28). *How Much Should I Charge as a Consultant? A Consultation Fee Breakdown*. Foundr. https://foundr.com/how-much-to-charge-for-consulting

Glassdoor. (2021a, April 17). Full Time Teacher Salaries. *Glassdoor*. www.glassdoor.com/Salaries/full-time-teacher-salary-SRCH_KO0,17.htm

Glassdoor. (2021b, May 23). Education Consultant Salaries. *Glassdoor*. www.glassdoor.com/Salaries/education-consultant-salary-SRCH_KO0,20.htm

Internal Revenue Service. (n.d.). *Self-Employment Tax (Social Security and Medicare Taxes)*. Internal Revenue Service. www.irs.gov/businesses/small-businesses-self-employed/self-employment-tax-social-security-and-medicare-taxes

KFOR Oklahoma's News 4 (Director). (2012). *Sweet Brown on Apartment Fire: Ain't Nobody Got Time for That!* [Film; Video]. www.youtube.com/watch?v=ydmPh4MXT3g

McIntyre, G. (2020). *What Percentage of Small Businesses Fail? (And Other Need-to-Know Stats).* Fundera. www.fundera.com/blog/what-percentage-of-small-businesses-fail

Pant, P. (2021, April 29). *How to Budget for Taxes as a Freelancer.* The Balance. www.thebalance.com/how-much-do-i-budget-for-taxes-as-a-freelancer-453676

Prakash, P. (2020, October 27). *Credit Card Processing Fees: The Complete Guide.* Fundera. www.fundera.com/blog/credit-card-processing-fees

Roddy, S. (2021, May 12). *How Do Small Businesses Approach the Budgeting Process?* Clutch. https://clutch.co/accounting/resources/why-small-businesses-need-budgets

Shulman, R. D. (2019, April 20). This Educator Made a Documentary about Teachers Turning Toward Entrepreneurship. *Forbes,* www.forbes.com/sites/robynshulman/2019/04/20/this-educator-made-a-documentary-about-teachers-turning-toward-entrepreneurship.

U.S. Small Business Administration. (n.d.). *Open a Business Bank Account.* U.S. Small Business Administration. www.sba.gov/business-guide/launch-your-business/open-business-bank-account

Weisner, Z. (2021, July 26). *7 Best Business Budget Software for 2021.* Fundera. www.fundera.com/blog/business-budget-software#one

Weiss, A. (n.d.). *Sample Proposals.* Alan Weiss. https://alanweiss.com/styles/pdf/Sample%20Proposals.pdf

6

Branding + Marketing

Knikole Taylor of Knikole Taylor Professional Learning Services, is a relatively new consultant who started her business less than five years ago. Nevertheless, she has had many opportunities to share her expertise with teachers all over the United States through virtual and in-person seminars, conferences and other events where she has proven to be a go-to resource on all things related to educational technology, especially Google tools. Her firm recently landed a highly competitive deal with Google to provide training services directly to its education customers. On the topic of branding and marketing, Knikole shared: "You have to be your biggest advocate. You have to be your biggest advertisement. You can't be afraid to toot your own horn. You can't be afraid to tell other people to toot your horn, as well! Otherwise, you won't get work."

What if the service you provide is exactly what an administrator, teacher, or other stakeholder needs to solve a difficult problem or to improve the work that they do? How will they know that you are out there and ready to serve them unless you make your presence known? As Knikole highlighted, your consultancy's survival relies on your ability to make others not only aware of what you have to offer, but motivated to hire you. This is the purpose of establishing a brand and marketing your business. Effective branding and marketing will solidify your professional reputation, amplify your unique skills and talents, and magnify awareness of your consultancy, ultimately resulting in an increase in leads and clients.

DOI: 10.4324/9781003172307-6

Your Brand Is More Than a Name

In his Forbes article, "What is a Brand Anyway?" Jerry McLaughlin, co-founder and CEO of Branders.com, defines "brand name" as "the name signifying the source of a product or service," and "brand" as "the perception customers have about that product or service." He also writes:

> Put simply, your "brand" is what your prospect thinks of when he or she hears your brand name. It's everything the public thinks it knows about your name brand offering – both factual (e.g. It comes in a robin's-egg-blue box), and emotional (e.g. It's romantic). Your brand name exists objectively; people can see it. It's fixed. But your brand exists only in someone's mind. Beginning in the later part of the 20th century, marketers began to grasp there was more to the perception of distinctive products and services than their names – something David Ogilvy described as the "intangible sum of a product's attributes." Marketers realized that they could create a specific perception in customers' minds concerning the qualities and attributes of each non-generic product or service. They took to calling this perception "the brand."
>
> (McLaughlin, 2011)

Do not confuse branding your business with giving it a name. You had to name your business to legally establish it, but with that, your branding journey has only just begun.

⊘ Check for Understanding: You Already Have a Brand

You may think that as a new entrepreneur, building your brand is like working on a blank slate. Since your business is just getting started, you may assume that prospective clients have no perception at all about your fledgling consultancy. This is probably not true. As a consultant, your reputation and your business's reputation are closely aligned. It is highly likely that in the early stages of your business, many of your customers will be your current and former employers, co-workers, students, and their parents. Many of your early referrals and leads will come from this network as well. So as you begin to think about how you want to brand your business, you may also want to consider your personal brand and how it will affect your entrepreneurial efforts.

How would your supervisors, colleagues, and other people you engage with professionally describe you? This is where your brand stands today.

 ## Do Now: Make a List, Build a Brand

How do you want your business to be perceived? Make a list of adjectives you would like others to use to describe your business. Remember your WHY as you complete this list, as it should align directly with the overall purpose of your business. In Table 6.1, you will find a sample list for your reference.

Table 6.1 Sample List of Branding Descriptors

• Reliable	• Attentive	• Friendly
• High-Quality	• Helpful	• Service-Oriented
• Punctual	• Supportive	• Caring
• Well-Prepared	• Insightful	• Professional
• Knowledgeable	• Fun	• Approachable

Extra Credit: Ask a Friend

Your brand is defined as how others perceive you, so you should enlist others to provide you with this valuable information. Interview several trusted colleagues, students, supervisors, or professors and ask them to provide you with a list of adjectives they would use to describe you. Analyze the results of this informal survey to identify trends. Are you happy with what people have to say? Are there some notably missing attributes that you would like to see? Record all of this information as you prepare to identify and establish a brand for your consultancy.

Market Your Business With Six Items

If your business's brand is how it is perceived by others, then marketing involves the strategies you adopt to make others aware of your business and its brand. Effective marketing not only increases recognition of you and your business, but it also motivates individuals, including those who do not have a direct connection to you, to research and procure your services.

Many consultants are able to build a clientele with little to no marketing, simply based on word-of-mouth and referrals. This can be a risky approach, particularly if you plan to become a full-time consultant. There are many steps you can take to be more proactive about publicizing your brand and the services you offer. Conversely, going overboard with marketing as a new consultant can be a big drag on your limited resources at a time in your business's growth when it is probably not necessary. Be careful not to invest too much time, and especially money, in marketing materials and plans. Here are six items the author recommends for a new educational consultant to effectively market their business:

1 Logo
2 Business card
3 Flyer
4 Website
5 Social media profile(s)
6 Mailing list(s)

Like many other aspects of your business, something is better than nothing when it comes to marketing. You may not have everything on this list when you are just getting started, and that is okay. Be intentional and frugal when making decisions about how to market your consultancy.

Your Logo = Your Name

A great logo can help to identify and distinguish your business. The easiest way to go about creating one is to simply turn your business name or even its initials into your logo. This is how each of the firms in Consulting Magazine's 2020 list of "Top 25 Consultants" went about making their corporate marks (Webb, 2021). If you decide to add a graphic element to your logo, make sure it is simple, modern, and reflects the values you want your brand to convey. You may want to employ a graphic designer to make your logo, if you can afford it. This would be a worthy investment, since your business's logo can appear on all marketing materials. A professionally-designed logo will make you look more professional! A great example of this is pictured in Figure 6.1, the professionally designed logo of Dr. Desiree Alexander, better known as "Educator Alexander."

If you cannot afford to hire a graphic designer, do not fret. According to Consulting.com: "Nobody is going to hire you based on your logo." (2019) This is especially true for educational consultants, who are often sought for their expertise and reputation. This means that while a logo can be part of your marketing strategy, it is by far, the least important part, and not worth a hefty investment of time or money in the earliest stages of your business. You

Market Your Business With 6 Items

1 **Logo**

Can be as simple as your business name or initials.

2 **Business Card**

Quickly and easily share your contact info.

3 **Flyer**

Useful when a potential client wants to know more about you than just your name and contact information.

4 **Website**

A place online for the public to contact you, learn more about your background and the services you offer.

5 **Social Media**

Share relevant, relatable content directly with your followers.

6 **Mailing List**

Stay in contact with individuals who have expressed an interest in your business.

Be intentional and frugal with your marketing decisions

Figure 6.1 Educator Alexander logo.

can make something yourself to use for now, and hire a designer to update it when your business grows and you can budget for the cost. It is easy for you to make a reputable logo by simply typing the name or initials of your business in a clean, professional-looking font and saving it as an image. If this strategy would be effective to create a logo similar to that of a prestigious, billion-dollar consulting firm like McKinsey and Company (look them up!) it should work for you and your business.

Always Carry Business Cards

Business cards may seem like a dated idea in the age of LinkedIn, Google search, and simply exchanging contact info via mobile phone. Nevertheless, some of the people you meet will prefer a printed, tangible reminder of who you are and what you do. You can quickly and easily share your contact information in a polished, professional manner with a business card.

Your business card should include:

◆ Your name
◆ Your business's name/logo
◆ Your title
◆ Preferred method of contact (business phone, email, or both)
◆ Web address

You may also decide to include a mailing address, but this is not absolutely necessary, especially if it is your home address. The author's business card is provided in Figure 6.2 for your reference.

According to best-selling author and entrepreneur, Kristopher Jones: "Business cards can still make a powerful impression on prospective clients. An email can be lost in a sea of spam and contact folders; a business card will remain in a client's wallet for years. Plus, if you're networking or giving

TINASHE BLANCHET
Principal Consultant
New Orleans, LA, USA

Keynote Speaker + Coach + Mentor
Edtech Support & Training
Google Certified Innovator + Trainer

Figure 6.2 Business card for Tinashe Blanchet & Associates. Contact info hidden for privacy.

an elevator pitch, it always helps to have the card" (Forbes Agency Council, 2021). What if a potential client sits next to you on an airplane or at a bar? You do not want to get caught scribbling your contact info on the back of a napkin! You should always keep a few of your business cards in your wallet for impromptu meetings, chance encounters and other unplanned interactions. You may also print extra business cards in batches as needed for conferences and other networking events.

Flyers – For When You Need More Than a Business Card

A flyer can be useful when a potential client wants to know more about you than just your name and contact information. It is also great to distribute to influencers, who may not be able to directly book your services, but can pass your information on to someone who can, a decision-maker. For example, if you are presenting at a conference, you may give each attendee a flyer that includes a professional photo of you, your bio and the services you offer in addition to your contact info. Decision-makers in your audience will now have all the information they need to book you, and influencers have information that they can pass on to a decision-maker. See Figure 6.3 for an example of a flyer used by the author. She saw a significant increase in leads and bookings when she distributed flyers instead of business cards at her seminars and conference sessions.

Put a few flyers in your laptop bag, backpack, or briefcase for when you meet someone who is really interested in your services and could benefit from having more information than what is included on your business card. Flyers can also be printed in small batches, specifically for presentations and other events where you have a captive audience. Distribute your flyer to individuals who request more information about your business. Also, do not hesitate

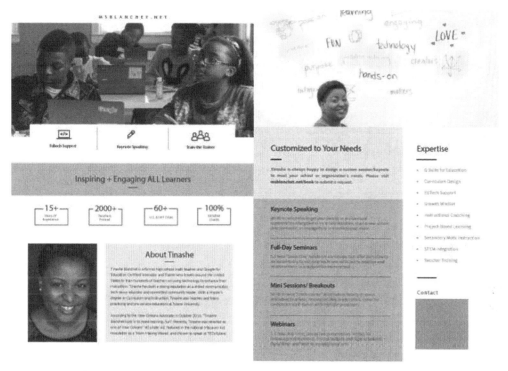

Figure 6.3 Flyer for Tinashe Blanchet & Associates (front and back). Contact info hidden for privacy.

to forward a PDF version of your flier to potential clients who reach out to you by email about your services.

Tech Tip: Use VistaPrint or Moo for Your Business Cards and Flyers

Like your logo, your business cards and fliers are not something you need to invest a lot of money into. However, it is important for your printed materials to give a great first impression, so you should avoid going the DIY (do-it-yourself) route. Websites like VistaPrint (vistaprint.com) and Moo (moo.com) are available for you to design and inexpensively print high-quality business cards and flyers. The author recommends VistaPrint for ease of use and affordable pricing and Moo for more creative design and high-quality printing options, like square and mini business cards. You should not print too many (>100) cards or flyers to start, as your contact information and messaging will surely change over time. You do not want to have a bunch of old materials to throw away when you make updates.

Your Business Needs a Well-Designed Website

In Chapter 4, "Establishing your Business (Paperwork + Incorporation)," one of the questions you were asked to answer was "How can your business be found on the internet?" However, from a marketing standpoint, your website is more than just another way for your business to be found. You must have a place online for the public to contact you and learn more about your background and the services you offer. A one-page site is fine to start with, as long as it includes the following information:

- ◆ Your business name and logo
- ◆ Your professional bio
- ◆ A list of the services you offer
- ◆ A contact form

Additional information including client testimonials, samples of your work, and a calendar of your availability can also be included. The author's website includes this and more and can be found at msblanchet.net.

Modern businesses must have a compelling web presence to compete in a marketplace where customers make many purchasing decisions based on information they find by searching the web. In a 2009 survey, 97% of buyers responsible for over $1.7 billion in professional services (primarily consulting) purchases said that a provider's website influenced their purchasing decision. According to marketing writer Jeanne Hopkins, "your website may very well be the most powerful tool in your marketing kit." She continues:

> It's clear that [consulting] firms must take advantage of this power. With well-designed websites they can:
>
> - ◆ **Establish that they are professional** : through professional design, writing, and arrangement of content.
> - ◆ **Establish that they are worthy of consideration** : through an overview of their services, their client list, biographies of their professionals, and case studies that show how they helped clients and delivered what they promised.
> - ◆ **Establish themselves as an authority** : through blog posts, publications, videos, and other resources to help build credibility, reliability, and trust- all essential elements necessary to win clients.
>
> (Hopkins, 2010)

The author built her own website using Squarespace (paid), and has also used WordPress (free) for previous versions of her blog and webpage. By the time this book is published, there will certainly be even more powerful web publishing tools available to readers that do not even exist at the time that this is being written! You can also hire a designer to build a website for your business. As previously mentioned in Chapter 4, you can always scroll to the bottom of your favorite website to find out who designed it or what publishing tool was used to create it.

Regardless of how you decide to go about building your web presence, the final product must be polished and consistent with your business's brand. The quality of your website matters. To quote the previous chapter: "You do not want to be viewed as a 'bargain-basement' consultant!" The easiest way to create a good website is to keep it simple. Adding too much information, and especially graphics, to your website can make it look cluttered and amateurish. In general, your website should be less decorative, and more informative. It should also be carefully edited and reviewed for spelling and grammatical errors. A web designer or marketing specialist can also help you optimize your site for accessibility and search engine optimization.

Personalize Your Brand With Social Media

Social media as we know it has only existed for less than 20 years, starting with Myspace reaching a million monthly active users in 2004. Nevertheless, it has changed our lives in irreversible ways, from how we communicate with our friends and family to how we entertain and inform ourselves. Social media platforms are used by one of every three people in the world, and more than two-thirds of all internet users. (Ortiz, 2019) For this reason, you must consider using social media to connect with potential clients and collaborators. On sites like Facebook, Twitter, and TikTok, you can share relevant, relatable content directly with your followers. With one "viral" post, you can increase your brand's visibility with a speed and magnitude unavailable on any other platform. Here is some advice shared in a Forbes article titled "How To Build A Brand Through Social Media":

- ◆ **Target the right platforms**. Not all social media platforms are created equal. Twitter is more of a conversation, best for sharing industry news or topics related to your brand. Facebook is similar to Twitter but with a much older audience. The key is to find the platform that will boost your profile and connect you with your target audience.

- **Build a brand voice**. Make sure that the images and content that you post is consistent with the style and imagery of your brand. Consider it like an advertising tool kit and keep it uniform across all platforms.
- **Post frequently (if possible)**. Post often to create engagement with your audience.
- **Create a unique hashtag**. It offers another way for people to find and share your work. Do your research and create a totally original hashtag.
- **Separate business and personal**. Unless you are a celebrity brand that is selling your lifestyle, it is better to keep the two separate and keep the attention on your brand message.
- **Connect with influencers**. Follow all the influencers in your industry and develop a meaningful conversation with them online. To get on their radar, comment and like their posts. Also post about their work and tag them. You can use DM's to make an initial connection, but be respectful and only reach out once.
- **Do it yourself**. Do your own social media so that it's your voice online, it's your voice DMing, and it is consistent when you meet in person. For a more authentic voice it is better to control your social media platforms.

(Bliss, 2019)

Build Your Audience With a Mailing List

Creating a mailing list will help you stay in contact with individuals who have expressed an interest in your business. Your first mailing list should be email – as this is the cheapest and easiest way for you to contact potential clients and other stakeholders. You could just start with a spreadsheet – make a list of the names and email addresses of people who you know would like to receive updates about your business – friends, family, and professional contacts. You can beef up your list by adding mailing list opt-in links to your website, social media and even your email signature. It is against the law to subscribe people to your mailing list without their consent. Make sure that you have an option for readers to unsubscribe from your emails. Free and low cost email services like Mailchimp (mailchimp.com) and Campaign Monitor (campaignmonitor.com) are available for you to manage your email lists, design and send emails, and view analytics to learn not only how many people are opening your emails, but what links they are clicking on, and more.

Try to send an email update or newsletter to your mailing list at least once a quarter. In this email, you could share updates about your services, helpful tips based on your expertise and, of course, promotional content for readers who may want to book your services. You also want to build a media contact list for sending press releases about awards you win, community service events, and other items you want to share with the public and news outlets.

Exit Ticket: Align Your Marketing with Your Brand

Now that you have an idea of what your brand is and how you can market your business, you should take some time to make sure that your marketing actually reflects your branding goals. For instance, if you want people to see your business as reliable, you may want to state on your website's contact form that you will follow up on contacts within one business day. Another example would be investing in a graphic designer and high-quality printing for your flyers and business cards, if you want to be viewed as a high-end, professional service provider.

Take a look at the adjectives you listed to describe your brand. How does your marketing incorporate these beliefs? Come up with a list of action items that will help you to more closely align your marketing tools and strategies with how you want your business to be perceived.

Extra Credit: Start Collecting Testimonials

Specifically ask satisfied clients, trusted colleagues, and esteemed supervisors to send you a written testimonial of your services. You can also invite individuals to review and rate your business on social media. These testimonials can also be shared on your website, social media profiles, in email newsletters, and even your flyer!

How do you research goods and services online? You probably look for reviews or testimonials from other buyers to help you make a decision. Even if you do not go on the web to make a purchase, friends and family can also weigh in on your choice. Success stories, positive reviews, and referrals from clients will surely help you to grow your business.

Chapter Review: Don't Be Afraid to Toot Your Own Horn!

Establishing a brand and marketing it effectively will often require you to step out of your comfort zone. As Knikole Taylor said: "Don't be afraid to toot your own horn!" Every interaction you have, not just in professional environments, but anywhere from the grocery store to your favorite restaurant, from the barber shop to the bus stop, is an opportunity for you to connect with a future client. As discussed in Chapter 3, do not let imposter syndrome or fear prevent you from sharing what you have to offer. If you want to master selling a product, you have to believe in it first. Guess what? As a consultant, YOU are the product that you are trying to sell. So building your brand starts with believing in yourself.

Get comfortable with having conversations in which you can discuss the benefits of your services in any setting, formal or informal, professional or personal. Keep printed marketing materials on hand at all times to share when prospects want to learn more about your business or contact you in the future. Proactively reach out to clients and leads on social media and through your mailing list. Your business's success depends on your ability to convince as many people as possible that your specific skills and expertise are an exact fit for their unique challenges and demands.

Reference List

Bliss, Sara. (2019, 13 February). How to Build a Brand Through Social Media. *Forbes*, www.forbes.com/sites/sarabliss/2019/02/13/how-to-build-a-brand-through-social-media/

Consulting.com. (2019). The Ideal Consulting Logo For 2019. *Consulting.com*, www.consulting.com/consulting-logo

Forbes Agency Council. (2017, 24 November). 2021 Is the Business Card Dead? 16 Experts Share Their Thoughts. *Forbes*, www.forbes.com/sites/forbesagencycouncil/2017/11/24/is-the-business-card-dead-16-experts-share-their-thoughts

Hopkins, Jeanne. (2010, 20 January). Research Shows Websites Influence 97% of Clients' Purchasing Decisions. *HubSpot Blog*, https://blog.hubspot.com/blog/tabid/6307/bid/5501/Research-Shows-Websites-Influence-97-of-Clients-Purchasing-Decisions.aspx

McLaughlin, Jerry. (2011, 21 December). What Is a Brand, Anyway? *Forbes*, www.forbes.com/sites/jerrymclaughlin/2011/12/21/what-is-a-brand-anyway

Ortiz, Esteban. (2019, 18 September). The Rise of Social Media. *Our World in Data*, https://ourworldindata.org/rise-of-social-media

Webb, Michael. (2021, 1 October). The Top 25 Consultants: The 2021 Honorees. *Consulting Magazine*, www.consultingmag.com/2021/10/01/release/

7

Communication + Project Management

Jeff Gargas is co-author of "Teach Better" and co-founder of Teach Better Team, a consultancy that develops training and resources for educators, schools, and districts. According to him: "It's ridiculously easy to start a business, but it's still really hard to maintain one!" As Jeff highlights, starting your consultancy is just the first, and arguably easiest, step towards making your business successful. It is not enough for you to simply provide your services, even if you do a great job at it. It is not even sufficient to make others aware of your work through branding and marketing. You must be able to follow up with prospects in a timely manner, provide them with all the information they need in order to secure your services and manage your responsibilities accordingly to make sure that each of your clients receives the appropriate amount of your attention and effort. Strong communication and project management is how you convert prospective clients to satisfied customers who will book you again and tell their friends and colleagues that they should book you as well. This is how your business goes from being new to tried and true!

Email Is Best, but Be Flexible

You can communicate with anyone in the world about your business instantly and inexpensively by email. An email conversation also provides written documentation of everything you discuss for future reference. It is a no-brainer that you should use this as your primary mode of contact, so much of the communication advice shared in this chapter will be regarding email.

DOI: 10.4324/9781003172307-7

However, you should always consider the needs of your clients and prospects when deciding how to communicate with them about your services. After an initial email, you may need to make a phone call or host a video meeting to discuss details before your contract is written and signed. Even if you are contracted to work, you may schedule another meeting to clarify expectations before an event or due date. Whatever it takes to make sure you and your client are on the same page is worth the effort. You can always send a confirmation email to document what was said over the phone or by webinar. Also, do not hesitate to deliver or send printed copies of any materials you would typically email for individuals who prefer having something "on paper." Your communication preference should never prevent you from communicating in ways that best suit your audience. Your clients and prospects will appreciate your willingness to connect with them in the manner they choose.

Remember the Four P's

Communication makes up a large part of the work you will do as a consultant. It is critical to your business's success that you communicate effectively. Try to keep the following four words in mind when you are communicating on behalf of your business:

1 Prompt
2 Purposeful
3 Proactive
4 Polite

Be Prompt: Convert Leads to Clients, Quickly

If someone is interested in you, but you do not follow up quickly enough, they can easily move on to another consultant, do the work themselves, or simply drop the inquiry. Research shows that minimizing your response time is particularly valuable for contacts via your website or an internet search. A Harvard Business Review study involving 1.25 million sales leads found that firms who tried to contact potential customers within an hour of receiving an internet-based query were more than 60 times more likely to "qualify the lead" than those who waited 24 hours or longer. "Qualify the lead" is defined as having a meaningful conversation with a key decision maker, which is exactly what you need to do to convert a lead to a client (Oldroyd et al., 2011).

Four P's of Effective Communication

Convert prospective clients to satisfied customers

Prompt

Try to reply within one hour or immediately with auto-reply.

Purposeful

Lead with the need. Don't expect anyone to listen or read without knowing why.

Proactive

Make it easy for them to say "yes." Don't leave out information that is likely to be requested.

Polite

Keep it kind and courteous. Don't communicate in a way that may reflect poorly on you or your business—*especially in writing!*

This reveals that timeliness in communication is not just a matter of respect; it can make or break your business! You do not want leads to go "cold," or to lose interest before you have a chance to respond.

✅ Check for Understanding: Running Late? Automate!

The idea of getting back to someone by phone or email even within one hour can seem nearly impossible, especially if you have a "day job" in addition to your business. Do not let your busy schedule prevent you from taking this necessary step. If you use a contact form on your website, set it up to automatically send an email or at least show a message on screen thanking the contact for completing the form and listing next steps, including exactly when they can expect a non-automated response from you. You may also set up your business voicemail to provide this information for individuals who contact you by phone. This ensures that prospects get an immediate response, increasing your chances at getting them to eventually book your services. See Table 7.1 for an example auto-reply message.

Table 7.1 Sample Auto-Reply Email for Online Contacts

> Thank you for contacting <business name>! This is an automatic response to let you know that your message was received. We will follow up with a more detailed response within 24 hours (excluding weekends).
>
> Please feel free to reply to this email if you have any additional information you would like to share, including the best way and time to reach you. Also see the attached flyer for more information about us.

Tech Tip: Make Sending Emails "Magical"

Magical (getmagical.com), formerly known as Auto-Text Expander, is a Google Chrome browser extension that enables you to create your own shortcuts that expand into full, frequently used text, from one word up to full paragraphs in Gmail, Outlook Web, and thousands of other websites and web apps. Rated as one of 100 "best free Google Chrome extensions" in 2021 by PC Magazine, Magical is a powerful tool for busy entrepreneurs to respond to emails in a timely manner. (Griffith, 2021)

The author uses Magical to quickly compose emails for responding to leads, scheduling appearances, securing contracts, and following up after work is completed. If she sends an email that may be copied and sent to someone else for the same purpose, she simply makes a shortcut

Table 7.2 Expanded Text from "joifwd" Shortcut in Magical

Hi <Client name>,
I would be happy to train your faculty. I am copying my assistant, Joi ******, so that she can follow up with you directly about scheduling and pricing. Looking forward to working with you!
Tinashe

Source: getmagical.com

for it. With Magical, you never have to write the same email twice! For example, the author often forwards email leads directly to her assistant, Joi. See Table 7.2 for an example of a message she composed to respond to these particular emails by simply typing the shortcut "joifwd" into a Gmail message.

 ## Do Now: Make an Email Template to Promptly Follow Up on Leads

When someone reaches out to you to learn more about your services, how exactly will you respond? Write a short email for this purpose right now, so that you can either automate it or quickly send it when necessary. If you have already started following up on leads by email, start with an email you have already sent for this purpose. You may want to edit it based on what you learn in this chapter, so stay tuned!

Be Purposeful: Lead With the Need

In a New York Times article aptly titled "Your Colleagues Don't Read Anything You Write. Here Are 8 Ways to Change That." Aaron Orendoff writes:

> Allow yourself to throw up a few first drafts in whatever form fits the need. . . . Then, flip it. Take the final sentence or paragraph and move it to the top. Rather than building to the request – and risk muddling the meaning – this inversion forces us to lead with the need.

Do you enjoy reading emails? How about receiving a marketing call? Probably not. With this in mind, be cognizant of how much time you spend getting to the point when you communicate with business contacts. Don't expect anyone to listen or read for too long without knowing why. Be straightforward and avoid "beating around the bush" with niceties or excessive details when making an ask in person or in writing.

If you are on a call or video meeting with a business contact, share what you hope to accomplish and next steps right at the beginning of the conversation. For example, you can start a meeting with a prospective client by saying: "I am hoping to answer all of your questions and pin down a date for training before we wrap up today. Then my assistant can send over a contract so we can get your date scheduled and confirmed. I am so happy to finally get a chance to meet with you!"

Use the subject line of your emails to clearly and succinctly establish the purpose of the communication or your "ask." If you need information or a task completed by a certain date, make sure you include this in the subject line. Also try not to put too much information in the email subject. Many individuals read email on their phones. On a phone screen, email subjects will get cut down to only a few words. See Table 7.3 for several sample email subjects that "lead with the need." Note that many of these include dates. If you need information or a task completed by a certain date, make sure you include this in the subject line.

Table 7.3 Purposeful Sample Email Subject Lines

• Remember to <specific task> by <date>
• Reminder of training on <date>
• Let's meet up! Please reply with availability
• Great meeting on <date>! I have a few questions.
• Do you need more information about ____?
• I need more information about _____ by <date>
• Please sign and return attached contract by <date>
• _____ attached. Feedback requested by <date>.

Be Proactive: Make It Easy for Them to Say "Yes"

The average American professional spends about 2.6 hours reading and responding to an estimated 120 messages received each day. (Plummer et al., 2019) Additionally, a recent survey of about 2,000 workers revealed that 67% of respondents believed they could not get their best work done due to excessive meetings (Hess, 2019). Your clients and prospects are probably bogged down with a barrage of emails and meetings. It is very easy for your pitch or request for information to get buried in this deluge. That is why it is so important to minimize the number of interactions between you and your business contacts by being proactive in your communication. Every time a prospective client has to reach out to you for more information, it adds to their workload. They may even get distracted and forget to follow up with you, reducing the chances of them actually booking your services.

Being proactive can simply mean to give a contact what they ask for before they ask for it. This may seem like a daunting task, but it is quite easy. All you have to do is pay attention. Never presuppose what a client wants or needs, as this will be different for each individual and organization. Making assumptions is not what being proactive is about. You will still need to ask questions and listen well to figure out the best approach for each interaction. The more you work, the more you will notice patterns in what clients need and which questions to ask to assess their needs.

Make it easy for prospective clients to say "yes" to your services. Take heed to what you get asked for the most and provide that information before it is requested. Here are a few tips and examples:

- ◆ Many prospects will ask for more details about you, your business, and the solutions you provide. You can attach an informational flyer to an initial email or direct prospects to your website to learn more about you after an initial meeting.
- ◆ The author noticed that after she invoiced clients, they almost always requested her IRS Form W-9 to forward to their accounting department to process payment. Accordingly, she now attaches her W-9 to all sent invoices.
- ◆ Send an email to meeting attendees (and absentees) with a recap of the agenda and a list of next steps. This may cut down on follow-up questions, especially from anyone who missed the meeting.
- ◆ When providing additional information in an email, try to do it as an attachment or a link, at the end of the email. You do not want to give them more to read!

Be Polite: Keep It Kind and Courteous

Considering the heavy workload your clients and prospects are undoubtedly dealing with, you will receive emails and calls that are aggressive or even downright rude. In the unforgettable words of Michelle Obama: "when they go low, [you] go high" (CNN, 2016). All communications from your consultancy should be as kind and courteous as possible. In general, when a client or prospect is disagreeable or simply slow to respond, it is not about you or anything you did wrong. On this topic, best-selling author and marketing expert Tim Grahl writes:

◆ Assume other people are busier than you.

◆ Assume that everyone's default behavior is to protect his or her time and workload, and that's ok.

◆ Assume that if they say "no" that it's for a very good, legitimate reason.

◆ Assume that if they ignore you that it's for a very good, legitimate reason.

(85)

Keep these edicts in mind when you communicate with clients and prospects. They are very busy and when they ignore or lash out at you, it is probably just a reflection of what they are dealing with in their own professional (or personal) life. Adopting this mindset will spare you a lot of anger and frustration when dealing with difficult clients. Nevertheless, you will certainly find yourself in situations where your ability to be polite will be greatly tested.

Do not communicate on behalf of your business when you are feeling exhausted, frustrated, or overwhelmed. It is okay to feel this way at times, but it is not okay to let these feelings affect how you respond to prospects and clients. Even if it negatively impacts your response time, it is better to wait than to communicate in any way that reflects your ill feelings and not your client's best interest. Additionally, try to avoid resolving disputes in writing. Ask if you can schedule a call or meeting to address concerns.

For example, let's say that you are publicly called out in a way that you believe is unfair, like with a negative review. Resist the temptation to respond publicly. It can appear that you are being defensive, and this will be off putting to others. Instead, reach out to the reviewer privately to schedule a call or video meeting. Then calmly discuss their grievances and try to find a way to resolve their issue. If you are able to come to an amicable agreement, you may even ask the reviewer to update their review to reflect the solution you provided.

Politeness is especially important when you are communicating online, in writing. Once you send an email or create an online post, you have absolutely no control over who gets to see it. It can be forwarded to anyone, anywhere! What is almost always a temporary moment of discord will be immortalized forever when you fire off an email or post in the heat of the moment. Even a subtly shady remark can turn a minor disagreement into an irreconcilable dispute. If you know that you are about to write something in anger, you may go ahead and write it, but do not send or post it right away. Instead, give yourself a day to cool off so you can go back and rewrite it when you are more calm. You may decide not to send it at all!

The Fifth P: Project Management

As your workload and clientele grows, your ability to adhere to the four P's in communication will heavily depend on a fifth P: project management. Successful project management will ensure that you communicate promptly, purposefully, and proactively. It will also mitigate frustration and overwhelm when dealing with competing priorities, supporting your need to be polite. In a Forbes article titled "What is Project Management Exactly?" Meredith Galante and Adam Hardy write:

> We all exercise our project management skills in everyday life. We run errands, complete DIY home improvement projects, plan parties and much more. In a business setting, project management looks different at every organization, but it always helps a team achieve a goal or solve a problem with a set deadline. . . . Project management is important in business because it helps you complete projects successfully and hit goals for yourself and your clients.
>
> (2021)

Project management is essential for large corporations and organizations that routinely provide services involving many tasks, constraints, and a large team of employees and stakeholders. As an independent consultant, often your "team" for a given project will only consist of two people, you and your client. Nevertheless, it is very easy for a client to "slip through the cracks" or get overlooked, even when you are just getting started. Project management broadens the scope of your work from the service you provide to the entire life cycle of each client relationship. You should have a system in place to track each prospect and where they are in this process from initial contact to completion and follow-up.

The author often uses spreadsheets to monitor correspondence and project goals. See Figure 7.1 for the spreadsheet she used to track communication with interviewees for this book, primarily using the "insert checkbox" feature in Google Sheets (instructions available at https://support.google.com/docs/answer/7684717). In the "Initial List" tab of this spreadsheet, she documented each consultant she contacted for an interview, noted who replied to her initial email, when they scheduled an interview date, and completed the interview. She also recorded who submitted a required release form to be quoted in the book and who referred someone else to be interviewed. There is also space for notes-important details that the author wanted to remember when working with each interviewee. The "Pre-Interview" tab at the bottom of the sheet links to data that is collected from a Google form on each

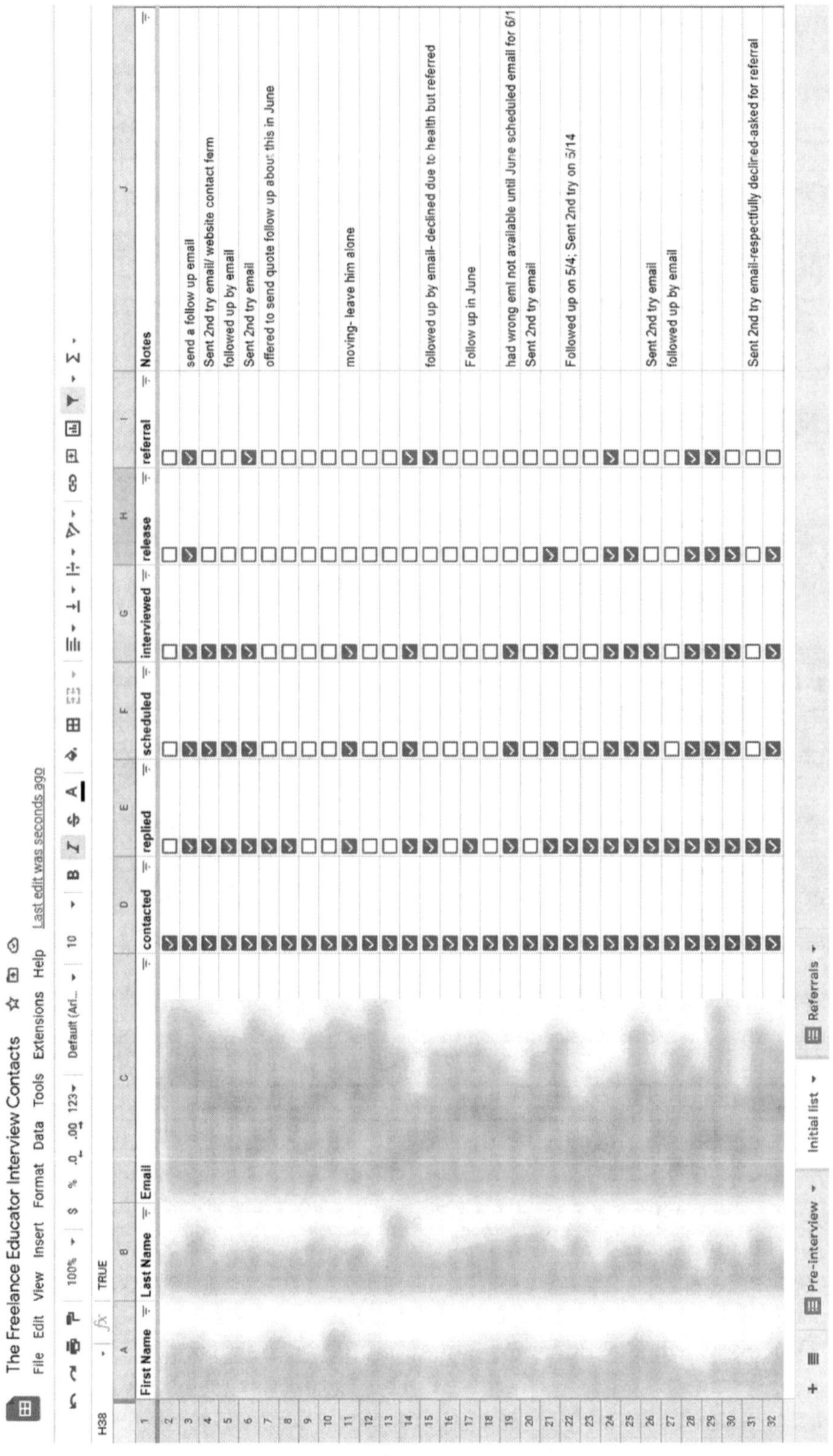

Figure 7.1 The Freelance Educator Interview Contacts Initial List tab. Contact information hidden for privacy.

confirmed interviewee. This is also where the author recorded notes from each interview. The "Referral" tab links to data from a referral form. This tab looks very similar to the "Initial List," but it connects each referral to the person who referred them.

Sometimes the author may create a custom spreadsheet for a long-term contract to document deadlines and deliverables to share with a client. This comes in handy when she needs to show evidence of services rendered over time. This spreadsheet can also be shared with collaborators who can track their progress towards delegated tasks. You can see an example of this in Figure 7.2. Here you will see a spreadsheet the author used to manage a district-wide, semester-long "Innovative Educator Cohort and Technology Grant" program in which teachers were recruited and vetted to participate, granted a suite of hardware and software tools, and trained to provide professional development on these tools for their peers. The drop-down feature in Google Sheets was used for this project to mark each task as "Not Started," "In Progress," or "Completed."

Exit Ticket: Project Management Spreadsheet Template

Visit bit.ly/freelanceduprojectsheet to create a project management spreadsheet. This template is an editable Google Sheet that you can use to get started with managing your clients' contact information, contract status, deliverable due dates, and more. If you prefer using Microsoft Excel, click "File"> "Download" > "Microsoft Excel (xlsx)." Remember to feel free to add or remove any columns to customize it for how you do business.

Chapter Review: The Teacher Is Now the Student

How many times have you asked a student to clean out their binder, backpack, or locker so they could be more prepared for your class? If you are a former teacher, then you surely worked with students who struggled not because they were incapable of doing their work, but because they were unorganized and thus unable to keep up with their assignments. You know how important it is for students to minimize clutter so they can have more time and energy to focus on their studies. Now it is time for you to put systems in place to free your brain (and email inbox) of the clutter that may keep you from offering the best possible service to your clients. Productivity guru and author of "Getting Things Done," David Allen, is famous for saying: "Your mind is for having ideas, not holding them" (2021). Creating a spreadsheet or

Task	Description	Notes	Links to Deliverables	Deadline	Status
Planning					
Application	Create Draft Google Form for application process	Fwd to ___ for final approval			Completed
Personal Statement ?s	Create Draft Google Form for application process				Completed
Info Sheet		Fwd to ___ for final approval			Completed
Talking Points					Completed
Recruitment					
Principal Email	Write email to principals				Completed
Notify Principals	Reach out to principals by email letting them know that this is coming	Tinashe will write email— Send			Completed
Informational Meetings	Schedule/ conduct 2 informational meetings before app is due	include meeting dates in application info			Completed
Press Release	Write press release	Fwd to [			Completed
Banner for Website		Create banner ; get dimensions form			Completed
Hardware Acquisition					
Finalize Items List	Follow up with ___ to finalize list of approved items/ budget	confirm with			Completed
Order Hardware	Order all teacher-issued devices in time for arrival before				Completed
Distribute Hardware	Distribute hardware to teachers ASAP				Completed
Selection					
Notify applicants of final status	Send email to awardees and decline letters to everyone else by COB Friday	Tinashe will write email—			Completed
Wrap-Up					
Cohort Initial Training	Plan and conduct full-day training for cohort members				Completed
Final Report	Submit project report to				Completed

Figure 7.2 Innovative Educator Cohort and Technology Grant Program Project Management Sheet. Links, names, and dates hidden for privacy.

using some system to monitor your progress saves you from having to juggle all of your to-dos in your mind. This will free you up to be more intentional in your communication and more creative in your approach to your work as an educational consultant.

Reference List

Allen, David. About. *Getting Things Done*, https://gettingthingsdone.com/about/. Accessed 4 December 2021.

CNN, director. (2016). *Michelle Obama's Entire Democratic Convention Speech*. YouTube, www.youtube.com/watch?v=8Tdl5NCJvuY.

Galante, Meredith, and Adam Hardy. (2021, 1 April). What Is Project Management, Exactly? Definitions, Tools, Techniques and More. *Forbes*, www.forbes.com/advisor/business/what-is-project-management/.

Grahl, Tim. (2020). *Your First 1000 Copies*. Edited by Leslie Watts, Story Grid Publishing LLC.

Griffith, Eric. (2021, 29 March). The Best Free Google Chrome Extensions. *PCMag*, www.pcmag.com/news/the-100-best-free-google-chrome-extensions.

Hess, Abigail J. (2019, 17 November). 67% of Workers Say Spending Too Much Time in Meetings Distracts Them from Doing Their Job. *CNBC*, www.cnbc.com/2019/11/17/67percent-of-workers-say-spending-too-much-time-in-meetings-distracts-them.html.

Oldroyd, James B., et al. (2011, March). The Short Life of Online Sales Leads. *Harvard Business Review*, https://hbr.org/2011/03/the-short-life-of-online-sales-leads.

Orendorff, Aaron. (2020, 9 March). Your Colleagues Don't Read Anything You Write. Here Are 8 Ways to Change That. *The New York Times*, www.nytimes.com/2020/03/04/smarter-living/your-colleagues-dont-read-anything-you-write-here-are-8-ways-to-change-that.html.

Plummer, Matt, et al. (2019, 22 January). How to Spend Way Less Time on Email Every Day. *Harvard Business Review*, https://hbr.org/2019/01/how-to-spend-way-less-time-on-email-every-day.

8

Why + How to Grow Your Business

Dr. Sarah-Jane Thomas founded the EduMatch project in 2014, which promotes connection and collaboration among teachers around the world. The EduMatch network has grown to include over 30,000 educators representing six continents. Through EduMatch Publishing, Sarah has also helped to elevate the authentic voices of educators in publishing over 80 books. How did she do it? According to Sarah: "From day one, I was very intentional with not using the word 'I', but using the word 'we'" Sarah's experience is very unique. Most of the consultants interviewed for this book are sole proprietors and many indicated that they struggled with figuring out why and how to grow their business. What you can learn from Sarah is that having the "we" mindset from the start is a powerful way to set your business up for future growth.

As an independent consultant, you are probably not ready to hire employees, as this entails myriad responsibilities, including added tax liability, managing benefits, and more. For this reason, guidance for hiring and managing employees is not included in this chapter. However, you are not in this alone. There are many individuals who will be inspired by your work and happy to help you bring your vision to the next level. In this chapter, you will learn all about growing your business from knowing when the time is right to seek assistance, how to get help, and how to grow your clientele.

DOI: 10.4324/9781003172307-8

What Is Your WHY?

As previously mentioned, working as an independent consultant is often a one-person endeavor and that is okay. Nevertheless, there are many reasons why you may decide to start building a team of individuals to represent your consultancy. Sarah's vision for EduMatch was rooted in a community mindset. Her mission and vision required her to build a team right from the start. Even if your "WHY" does not immediately call for assembling a group of collaborators, you may find that as your clientele and workload grows, your ability to deliver services in a way that aligns with your mission and vision may diminish over time. If you have a "day job," this may happen more quickly than you expect. Depending on your workload, you may realize that you need help right from the start.

Growing your business may simply mean bringing others in to do the things you do not want to do or are unable to do. Dr. Mary Howard is a literacy expert and author who has worked full-time as an independent educational consultant for over 25 years. She shared some advice she got from her brother: "You do what you're good at and you pay people to do what you're not." Maybe branding and marketing is not an area in which you feel comfortable. Like many educational consultants, you may struggle with managing money. Sending invoices, negotiating contracts, submitting tax forms, and other tedious, yet essential tasks associated with your business are probably not a part of your "WHY," or the reason you started your consultancy. More importantly, it is unlikely that you are an authority in any of these areas. There are plenty of individuals and organizations who can provide expert advice and support for any aspect of your business that you may need help with.

In Table 8.1, you will find a list of individuals you may decide to hire to get expert assistance for your business.

Table 8.1 Who to hire for expert assistance

• Accountant/bookkeeper
• Business attorney
• Marketing consultant
• Graphic designer
• Social media consultant
• Small business consultant/coach

When you start to have difficulty managing incoming leads, due to increased volume, or just a lack of skill or motivation in this area, your growing business is in danger of becoming stagnant. You do not want to lose work because you cannot handle it all. Paradoxically, you may find that you must grow your business in order for your business to continue to grow!

When You Can't Do It All Yourself: Hire a Virtual Assistant

One of the easiest and most affordable ways for you to get the help you need with the everyday work of running your consultancy is to hire a virtual assistant (VA). According to a U.S. Chamber of Commerce article titled "Virtual Assistants: What They Do, and How to Decide if You Need One":

> A virtual assistant is an individual who provides administrative services to clients while working from a remote location. Virtual assistants are often independent, self-employed contractors, though you can also work with a virtual assistant agency. Additionally, many candidates have a few years of experience as an administrative assistant or office manager in a professional office setting. . . . One of the major advantages of hiring a virtual assistant is [that] small businesses can select and pay for the specific services they need.
>
> (Peek, 2020)

What Can a Virtual Assistant Do for You?

A great assistant will manage logistics, giving you more time and energy to commit to delivering high-quality consulting services. When you hire an assistant, you will have to decide which tasks you feel comfortable with outsourcing to a third party. Here is a (partial) list of what a VA can do for you:

- Answer emails/phone calls
- Scheduling/manage your calendar
- Send invoices
- Collect payments
- Negotiate contracts
- Follow up and outreach
- Manage subcontractors

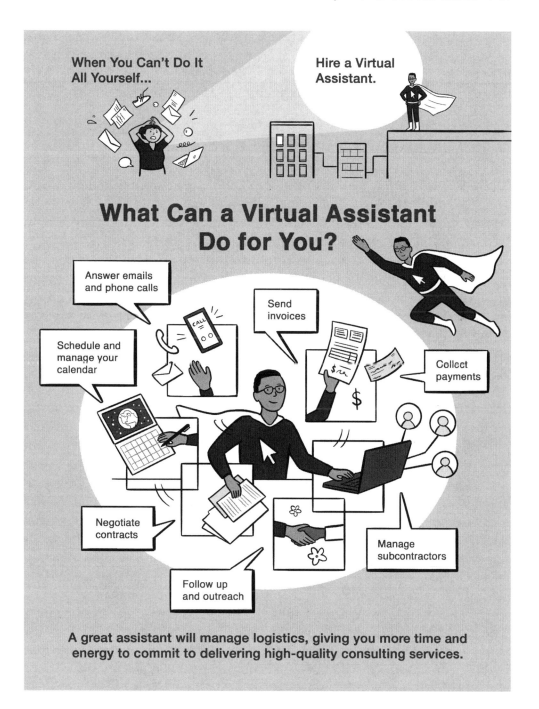

VAs can also book travel, conduct research, and even file business paperwork on your behalf. Of course, you are in total control of which tasks you choose to delegate. As your relationship with your assistant evolves over time, you may trust them to do even more as a representative of your business.

⊘ Check for Understanding: "I Can't Afford an Assistant!"

At this point, you may be thinking: "I can't afford an assistant!" although you could use the help. Beware of trying to save money by hiring someone who lacks significant (>5 years) experience in providing administrative services. In most cases, you will get what you pay for. An experienced VA is not a "gopher." They will bring a level of expertise to your consultancy that has the potential to transform how you do business. Toya Imani, business director of Imani Enterprise Virtual Services, shares this advice for finding an affordable VA: "Most virtual assistants offer at least a few packages based on your business's needs, including pay per hour. Choose the package that best fits your budget." With over 20 years of customer service experience, Toya knows that her clients value the professionalism and top-notch support she and her team provide.

The average educational consultant makes about $5,500 per month (Glassdoor, 2021). The average pay for a VA is $16.14 per hour, with VAs typically earning up to $25.70 per hour. (Payscale, 2021) This means that you could probably find a VA to do up to 20 hours of work per month for less than $500, or about 9% of an average educational consultant's pay. With a VA, your consultancy will no longer be average! Expect to see an increase in your productivity, and thus, your income, soon after you bring a VA onto your team.

For example, the author hired her assistant, Joi Guillory of Array Virtual Business Solutions, based on a friend's referral. The author was unable to respond to prospects in a timely manner, mainly when she was traveling for work. As a sales professional with over 18 years of experience, Joi was not only able to take over clerical tasks, but she also became an indispensable resource for sales and marketing advice. Joi is also a master at dealing with money, negotiating rates, and collecting payments, an area in which the author lacks confidence and experience. With Joi's help, she successfully doubled her consulting rates and greatly increased her clientele in less than two years. Before you rule out getting a VA as something that is not in your budget, you may want to consider this: if your business is growing at a rate that you are struggling to keep up with, you cannot afford to *not* get some help.

Do Now: Find a Virtual Assistant

Nationally-recognized financial expert and journalist, Miranda Marquit writes:

> One of the best ways to find a virtual assistant is to ask for recommendations. Many freelance VAs work for multiple clients, so you can ask people in your network whether they know someone. . . .
>
> Once you have a solid list of names and resumes, choose three or four to interview. Get a feel for how they operate and whether their style matches yours. Get some references and check up on them. Remember – a VA is going to represent you in some fashion. . . . You want to make sure they're professional and can accurately represent you.
>
> (2021)

Start researching VAs for your consultancy today. Even if you are not yet ready to hire someone, you can benefit from having a few individuals to contact if and when you need to get some help with your business. As you begin your search, also keep in mind that you are not bound by geography. Joi is based in New Orleans, yet she serves clients across the U.S., from California to Pennsylvania. Imani Enterprise is based in Houston and has served clients in Atlanta and the Washington, D.C. area. VAs provide services remotely, which means that you can find someone to assist you who lives in a different city, state, or even country from where your business is located.

 Tech Tip: Find a VA on the Web

Check out the following list of websites and social media networks you can use to find a VA:

- ◆ Upwork.com
- ◆ Fiverr.com
- ◆ Remote.co
- ◆ LinkedIn
- ◆ Facebook Groups
- ◆ Twitter

Interns: Nice to Have, but Not Necessary

Free help may be available to you in the form of an intern, or a student who will work with you to get practical experience. Interns can help with research, social media, marketing, outreach, and more. Connect with your local universities and community colleges to learn about recruiting interns for your business. Sometimes you can get a professor to send students from their course to work with you to earn college credit. You may even be asked to provide feedback on their performance that could impact their grade. It is most ideal for students to be accountable in some way for the work they do for you, since you are not paying them.

Not every intern will work at a level commensurate with your expectations. They are still learning! This is why you should try to avoid assigning essential tasks to interns. For instance, you may not depend on your intern to follow up on leads, as this is an essential task. If your intern forgets to do this or does it improperly, it can do irreparable damage to your business's reputation. Instead, you may ask an intern to draft a message template you can use to respond to leads quickly. This will give you an opportunity to review it before sending it out. If it does not get done, or is not done well, you still have a chance to do it or correct it at no risk to your business.

Also keep in mind that every intern has an expiration date. You may only have them for a few months while they are enrolled in a certain course. Sometimes they may switch courses, majors, or even schools, which may result in your losing them unexpectedly on short notice. It is totally possible for you to develop a great working relationship with an intern you can trust who will offer their free assistance for an extended amount of time. Nevertheless, they will eventually graduate from school and move on to a paid position. The transient nature of intern relationships is another reason for you to avoid delegating core functions of your business to an unpaid college student. Interns are nice to have, but you should not set up your business such that they are necessary for you to operate effectively.

Expand Your Reach With Subcontractors and Referrals

In an article titled "Use Subcontractors to Build Your Business," Entrepreneur Magazine shares, "For some companies, hiring subcontractors can be a stop-gap measure to handle big projects or get through busy periods; for others, it's a long-term strategy designed to create a scalable organization at minimal cost" (Resnick, 2021).

When you are too busy or unqualified to take a gig, you can reach out to someone who you trust personally and respect professionally to do the work. Hiring them as a subcontractor means that they can work on behalf of your company, and you get to share the revenue generated from the services rendered, although you did not render them yourself. Subcontractors enable you to expand your consultancy's offerings and increase your income while minimizing your added workload and cost. Nevertheless, subcontractors do require oversight. Your subcontractor agreement must be very clear and of course, in writing. You may hire a lawyer to help you draft an agreement to make sure your interests are protected.

In the aforementioned article, Rosalind Resnick writes:

> While many subcontractor relationships begin with a handshake, it's important to put each specific project in writing before you get too far down the road. One reason is obvious: taxes. Unless you're spoiling for a fight with the IRS, you need to specify in writing that your subcontractors (whether they're individuals or other businesses) aren't employees and that they're responsible for paying their own taxes and benefits.
>
> You'll also need to spell out the subcontractor's responsibilities, payment rate (project or hourly), and deadlines. Your agreement letter should also contain a provision allowing your company or the contractor to terminate the contract upon giving a certain amount of notice – 30 days, for example. If the contractor doesn't carry his or her own liability insurance, you should call your own insurance company to see if [they] can be added to your policy.
>
> (2021)

You may not be ready to take on the responsibility of hiring and managing subcontractors, and that is okay. Another way to grow your business is to develop relationships with other consultants and consultancies to whom you can refer clients when you are unable to deliver services yourself. Your prospects will appreciate your assistance and may return to you with future inquiries.

Upselling, Cross-Selling, and Service Contracts

If you effectively incorporate the strategies shared in Chapter 6, "Branding + Marketing" and Chapter 7, "Communication + Project Management," you may need other individuals to help you manage your workload from incoming leads. Most of the advice shared in this chapter is regarding ways to increase your capacity when your clientele and duties grow to a point that you cannot deal with alone. However, once you get the help you need, you may find yourself in a position where you are ready to handle even more work. In addition to marketing, communication and project management, here are some strategies you can adopt so that you can increase your income and impact.

According to the Harvard Business Review, "acquiring a new customer is anywhere from five to 25 times more expensive than retaining an existing one" (Gallo, 2014). Sales and marketing professional J.T. Rimbey offers a very straightforward explanation of upselling and cross-selling:

> [U]pselling and cross-selling is a far more profitable way to grow your business. . . . Not only can upselling and cross-selling to customers be a great opportunity for you, but it also works to help your customers and maintain their trust. In fact, upselling has less to do with pushing more goods and services on a customer, and more on focusing to meet your customer's needs.
>
> **Upselling** is a sales technique where the customer is offered a higher priced option or add-on to the product they are purchasing. Examples of an upsell could be introducing a larger screen to a customer looking at televisions or adding a warranty to the product being sold.
>
> **Cross-selling** is offering a complementary product or service that the original product does not cover. For example, offering a credit card to a customer that is opening a checking account. They are related, but not overlapping, products that the customer might find useful. . . .
>
> The most well-known example to show the distinction between upselling and cross-selling is McDonald's. "Would you like to Supersize that?" is a classic upsell, while "Would you like fries with that?" is a cross-sell. One is adding to the product you have, while the other is offering a completely different, but complementary, product.
>
> Another example is the airport. An upsell is upgrading from economy to first class. A cross-sell is the food and headphones that they offer for sale on the plane. Upselling, then, requires convincing the customer of the added value of a higher-priced item. Cross-selling means finding [additional] products that will enhance your customer's experience.
>
> Upselling and cross-selling are closely related and useful in both increasing your profit and anticipating your customer's needs. In order to be successful, though, you must thoroughly understand what

your customer is looking for and offer them products [or services] at the appropriate time that demonstrate your understanding.

(Rimbey, 2019)

If you are asked to host a short training, you may upsell by offering to conduct a longer session or a series of short sessions. The advantage of this is simply that you have more time to go in-depth with whatever topic you are presenting on. The author often cross-sells a follow-up Q&A webinar session with a scheduled in-person training event. Although this will increase the client's investment, it will also enhance the overall value of their purchase. Teachers really appreciate knowing that they will have a chance to ask questions and get targeted assistance after they attend a training.

Service contracts with consulting clients are a way to make sure their needs are met while securing a steady stream of income for your business over a set amount of time. When clients ask for services that are outside of the scope of what you can do in a single appearance or event, do not try to convince them to scale back their ask. Instead, you can offer to extend the length and/or scope of your agreement so that you can thoroughly meet their request at an increased total cost. You may even offer a "discounted bulk rate" to make your pitch more appealing. For example, if you charge $3,000 for a one-day training, offer to do a series of four quarterly sessions at a "discounted bulk rate" of $10,000!

Your responsibilities under a service contract can be very broad, so be sure to specifically list expectations and deliverables in the contract or in an attached description of services. See Table 8.2 for an example of a description of services.

As you approach the completion date of an established service contract, begin to assess client needs that you can address under a subsequent agreement. Discuss these next steps with your client before the end of your contract in an effort to get another agreement started once the existing one ends. Establishing a few long-term contracts can help stabilize your income and remove some of the unpredictability that often typifies being an independent contractor. Working repeatedly with a client and providing services that consistently meet their needs is not only financially rewarding, but it also helps them accomplish their goals and enhances your business's professional reputation.

Exit Ticket: Dare to Dream! Again!

In Chapter 2, "Writing a Business Plan," you were presented with one of many "Do Now" activities included in this text: "Give yourself at least 15

Table 8.2 Description of Services for Innovative Educator Cohort

Objectives

1 To provide up to twenty-five (25) hours of professional development that increases and optimizes tech use for teachers and administrators across the [organization name removed for privacy].

2 To provide up to fifteen (15) hours of support to the Innovative Educator Cohort (IEC) members of [organization name removed for privacy].

Total Contracted Time: 40 hours

Meetings

- The assistance in achieving the objectives would include, but not be limited to, the following activities:

- Monthly Group facilitation of informational meetings and/or one-on-ones with cohort members. In accordance with IEC requirements, cohort members agreed to scheduled monthly cohort meetings from 4:30 to 6:00 p.m. on the following dates:

- Thursday, November 10

- Wednesday, December 14

- Thursday, February 9

- Future monthly meeting dates, times, and locations will also be determined based on cohort members' availability.

- Group observation and feedback, with recommendations on how to improve technology professional development for teachers moving forward.

- Up to 25 hours of professional development will be provided based on agendas, dates, times, and locations agreed upon by me and a representative of your organization.

Timing

I'm available to work with you November 8 – April 30.

Terms and Conditions

My fees are always based upon the project, and never upon time units. While the PD hours are limited to 40, feel free to call upon me for consultation or advice without worrying about a meter running. I'm happy to suggest additional areas of focus without concern about increasing your investment.

The fee for the assistance detailed above would be $ payable upon completion of this contract on May 1.

minutes to come up with a clear vision, in your mind's eye, of what your ideal business would look and feel like. Write down as much of what you envision as you can. Treat this like a brainstorming exercise – do not worry about complete sentences or correct grammar. Just capture as much as possible. You can use this as a reference tool when you finally write a formal business plan."

You may still have yet to write a formal business plan! Nevertheless, take a moment to close your eyes and envision your business, again. Brainstorm about everything you have learned from reading this book. Surely your vision is different based on what you now know.

Extra Credit: Did You Make a Vision Board Yet?

If not, now would be a great time to do it! If so, take a look at it and consider making some additions (or omissions) based on your renewed vision. See Chapter 2 for more about vision boarding.

Chapter Review: A Good Problem to Have

A 2021 Forbes article lists five common growing pains experienced by small businesses:

1. Constantly putting out fires
2. Not enough time to meet business demands
3. No processes
4. Ineffective communication
5. Knowing when to scale (Yoon)

While you may feel plagued by one, two or even all five of these issues, having them means that your business is on a growth curve. You may find yourself feeling frustrated or overwhelmed by problems that did not exist when you only had a few clients to worry about and no one to manage. The next time you feel this way, make sure you take a moment to reflect on how far you have come from the day you decided to start a business. Do not let the challenges of having a growing business prevent you from feeling proud and excited about what your consultancy is actually doing right now: growing!

Reference List

Gallo, Amy. (2014, 29 October). The Value of Keeping the Right Customers. *Harvard Business Review*, https://hbr.org/2014/10/the-value-of-keeping-the-right-customers.

Glassdoor. (2021, 4 December). Salary: Education Consultant. *Glassdoor*, www.glassdoor.com/Salaries/education-consultant-salary-SRCH_KO0,20.htm.

Marquit, Miranda. (2021, 13 May). What Is a Virtual Assistant? It's My Secret to a Thriving Business. *FinanceBuzz*, https://financebuzz.com/what-is-a-virtual-assistant.

Payscale. (2021, 22 November). Virtual Assistant Hourly Pay. *Payscale*, www.payscale.com/research/US/Job=Virtual_Assistant/Hourly_Rate.

Peek, Sean. (2020, 4 June). Virtual Assistants: What They Do, and How to Decide If You Need One. *US Chamber of Commerce*, www.uschamber.com/co/run/technology/what-is-virtual-assistant.

Resnick, Rosalind. Use Subcontractors to Build Your Business. *Entrepreneur*, www.entrepreneur.com/article/81358. Accessed 5 December 2021.

Rimbey, JT. (2019, 21 September). The Importance of Upselling and Cross-Selling in Sales. *Map My Customers*, https://mapmycustomers.me/blog/the-importance-of-upselling-and-cross-selling-in-sales/.

Yoon, Jennie. (2021, 20 July). Got Business Growing Pains? Here's How to Solve Them. *Forbes*, www.forbes.com/sites/theyec/2021/07/20/got-business-growing-pains-heres-how-to-solve-them.

Epilogue

A Word from the Author

When I began writing this book, I was still a full-time entrepreneur, running both my educational consulting business as well as a non-profit organization I founded. Both businesses were doing quite well, then my 20-year marriage ended abruptly and I became a single mom of three teenagers. It was difficult, but I kept both businesses afloat. Then the COVID-19 pandemic hit two years later, ending my ability to work with children and teachers in-person. For about a year, I pivoted, offering online summer programs through the non-profit and managing an unprecedented influx of webinar training requests on educational technology. Nevertheless, my non-profit did not survive the pandemic.

Neither did my educational consulting business. Maybe I could have made it work. But instead, I entered a new relationship, relocated to a new state, and decided to take a full-time position with one of my long-time consulting clients. This enables me to continue to do the work that I love (and am pretty good at), helping educators, while taking a break from the ups and downs of running two businesses. Being an employee means I also have more time to be a mom to my children, who will all be grown-ups much too soon.

I wanted to share this because I think that it is important for you, the reader, to understand that the best part of being a "freelance educator" is being free! Free to use your teaching and learning expertise in any way you choose. Free to call the shots at the helm of your own consultancy. Free to build your business in whatever way you see fit. Free to change your mind and your path any time you wish. In my own journey as a teacher, entrepreneur, and now author, I am often reminded of the saying: "you are a human being, not a human doing." No matter what I decide to do, I know who I am.

I am a master teacher. I am a lifelong learner. The world is my classroom.

I have worked in many capacities, often naively thinking that whatever job I was doing at the time would be my last. I now know that my talents and interests are quite broad, so my professional life appropriately reflects this. As an educator, I measure my success by the learners I impact. I am happy to say that every position I have held from high school teacher to college instructor, from non-profit founder to international speaker, has given me the opportunity to positively change the way children learn. For that, I am humbled and grateful.

I am even more grateful that I now have a chance to share what I've learned with you. In this book, I did my best to cover all of the logistics of starting a business – from a teacher's perspective. This text takes you through the necessary steps to get started with your educational consultancy. What makes an educational consultant great? I think I may need to answer that question in another book! Stay tuned.

Many of the educational consultants interviewed for this book talked about the importance of self-care. As an entrepreneur, it is very easy for you to become a workaholic, putting the success of your business above all – your relationships, your family, even your own health and well-being. Remember to take care of yourself. If you have to travel, schedule a sightseeing trip, even if it's on the way to the airport. Exercise in the hotel gym. Schedule a spa treatment. Binge a season of your favorite show or go out for a fancy dinner. Celebrate your successes. Treat yourself!

Even if you choose to keep your "day job," or like me, get a new one, you will be forever impacted by the people you meet, the places you go, and the experiences you have as an educational consultant. Your entrepreneurial journey will be exciting and challenging. Other educators will be inspired by your leadership and vision. Although you have come to the end of this text, it is very likely that your story, like mine, is just beginning. No matter where you are on your journey as an educational consultant, there is always more to learn and more to experience.

Educationally yours,

Tinashe Blanchet
The Freelance Educator